Understanding Business: The Logic of Balance

Understanding Business:
The Logic of Balance

Part of the Understanding Series of Books

Gary Moreau

ISBN-13: 9781547074730
ISBN-10: 1547074736
Library of Congress Control Number: 2017909124
CreateSpace Independent Publishing Platform
North Charleston, South Carolina

Contact: gary@gmoreau.com

In memory of John F. Meier (1947–2017). I blame him for nothing I write here, but I credit him for showing the rest of us how a good and honorable life is lived.

About the *Understanding* Series

Like all book series, the *Understanding* series began as a single title. I was an American living and working in Beijing, China, and struggling to understand the why behind the what of Chinese culture. I knew what to expect in most social and business settings. The differences between Chinese and Western culture were sometimes a source of stress, however, because I failed to grasp the motivation behind the behaviors that were at odds with my familiar Western conventions.

Motivation, I realized, is the context within which behavior occurs. It doesn't change the behavior that we may find unsettling. It somehow makes it less personal, however. And that makes the behavior, if not more acceptable, at least understandable. And with understanding, I have found, comes tolerance. It's not about me, after all.

And so my journey began. Eastern philosophy and religion are both pretty well documented, so that seemed a good place to start. And as I sought to understand both and how they differed from their Western counterparts, I inevitably found myself enwrapped in issues of reason and logic. Aristotle and Confucius, among many others, joined my trek, and their whispers eventually led me to the land of duality that is deductive and inductive logic.

And then it clicked. "Two" is a recurring theme throughout all of life. It takes two to make a pair. It takes two to make a baby. It takes two to tango. We have two hands, two feet, and two eyes. We experience highs and lows. We are happy and sad. We become ill and get better again. We record our commerce with double-entry accounting. There is sunshine, and there is shadow. The workweek has a beginning and an end. We live, and we die. We start a thought, and then, hopefully, we finish it.

All of a sudden, twos were everywhere I looked. And being in China, at the time, I didn't have to look far to see perhaps the most well-known symbol of two on the planet—the symbol known as Tài jí tú, the Great Polarity, or simply the symbol of yin and yang. In the Chinese world view, they are the two opposing but complementary forces that define the universe and everything in it.

When I moved back to the United States, the symbol of Tài jí tú itself was in less evidence. But the concept behind it remained everywhere. I continued to see twos in business, politics, parenting, and friendship. Light and dark. Fire and water. Male and female. Pro and con. Friendly and not. Good and bad. Hot and cold. And, yes, yin and yang.

The earth has two poles. A pole has two ends. An end once had a beginning. And the beginning of anything eventually comes to an end. The finish of one day leads to the start of a new one. A seemingly dead plant comes alive with the arrival of spring. Spring turns to summer. The circle of life turns.

The *Understanding* series is all about twos. Specifically, it is my attempt to use the duality of reason, deductive and inductive logic, to better understand both the world we live in and the pursuits we engage in while doing so. It is not a series devoted to philosophy or logic, although both can be found in some of the words and between them all for those so inclined to look.

It is a series devoted to the black and white of reality, recognizing that reality always takes on tangible dimension in a broader conceptual context. Nothing exists in isolation. Even absolutes are inevitably relative to something. A line bends back on itself to become a circle.

All shapes have a center of balance. An idea sparks new ideas. An understanding is both a beginning and an end.

If this all sounds boringly academic, let me assure you this is the one and only stop for that train. I am a sexagenarian now, living in the United States and consuming all of the reality I can get. I have enjoyed some taste of success and endured several helpings of failure. I have, however, been blessed with an interesting life overall. I've pursued my vocation of business on six continents. I've met royalty, both figurative and literal. I've had to reinvent myself a few times along the way, and I've suffered my share of chumps and fools.

And there you have it. The whole enchilada. The beginning, the end, and everything in between.

Enjoy the journey.

Gary Moreau

Foreword

A contrary perspective is a different perspective. The contrarian sees things quite apart from the accepted norm. Contrarians, as a result, can be viewed as insightful pioneers or just troublemakers, who like to stir the pot for their own entertainment. And, of course, they can be both. There is nothing to say a troublemaker can't tell the truth or provide a worthy service.

The difference between the prophet and the simply combative is context. Nothing happens in isolation. Context is everything. Context is the ecosystem in which beliefs exist. It is the context that ultimately sustains the belief or proves it wrong.

While the word "context" does not appear in the title, this book is all about context. Context is like that. It is often overlooked in debates over truth and lies because it impersonalizes observation and insight, and to paraphrase Sigmund Freud (1856–1939), all of life is personal.

The context I explore most diligently is the context of reason and logic. It is here that truth is often revealed. It is here that purpose and its influence are laid bare.

I am a contrarian. I admit to that. But I have context for what I believe. And while many of those beliefs are at odds with the accepted wisdom that has defined the corporate world in which I have toiled for the last forty years, it is the exploration of context that will be this book's greatest contribution, should it ultimately make any.

You may not agree with some of my observations and conclusions, although I wager that you will ultimately accept more than you may now think. That's okay. The exploration of reason and context are inevitably productive in their own rights. There are always insights to be gained, whether they lead to an epiphanic moment or simply validate existing conviction.

If you would like to get your career or business on track for success, I will do my humble best to help you on your way. And since the journey through the land of logic and reason is always its own reward, you really have nothing to lose.

One

The Need for Balance

The common beliefs and behaviors that define a culture arise out of the expectation that those beliefs and behaviors will lead to an anticipated result. Those expectations, however, are greatly influenced by our past experience—or, more precisely, how we define that past experience and its cause.

Reality is not absolute. You have only to pay a brief visit to wherever it is you get your news to see the extent of this truth. There would not be so much division and discord in the world if we all interpreted reality in the same way.

But we don't. Each of us filters reality through our own personal world view, our own personalized context within which we come to understand the world around us. In the end, we see what we expect to see. Or, more rigorously, we see what we allow ourselves to see.

It all began with the ancient Greek philosopher and scientist, Aristotle (384 BC–322 BC), who gave us formal logic. Specifically, he gave us deductive logic, the process by which we take a theory or series of observations and attempt to deduce a specific conclusion. It is a linear process that moves from left to right conceptually.

The scientific method is the best example of deduction at work. It is not a body of knowledge per se. The scientific method is a process for interpreting reality in a deductively sound way through controlled experimentation.

The monotheistic religions are also very deductive. Cause and effect. You behave in a certain way and believe certain things out of the expectation that those behaviors and beliefs will lead to an attractive outcome (e.g., heaven).

Most contemporary Western business practices, like the monotheistic religions that have historically defined much of Western culture, are likewise built on a foundation of deductive logic. We mine data and observation to formulate theories that are then expressed through specific policies, procedures, and actions in the hope of a specific and desirable outcome.

Eastern religions and cultures, in contrast, tend to be built on the conceptual foundation of inductive logic, which starts with a specific observation and speculates causation. This is a far more circular logic, as compared to the linear logic of deductive reason, and supports the dualistic nature at the heart of Eastern philosophy.

Taoism (also called Daoism), which has had a tremendous influence on Chinese and other Eastern cultures, is built around the core belief that the universe is simply too complex for the human mind to comprehend. It is an inductive conclusion not borne out by science or experimentation.

Similarly, Confucius (551 BC–479 BC), the famous Chinese philosopher, teacher, and political advisor, sought to instill social and political order through a matrix of rituals and obligations designed to internalize personal behavior that would support a progressive political state. Those rights and obligations, in other words, were induced from the desired state.

In the West, of course, social order is accomplished through the broad acceptance of the absolute moral code at the heart of all monotheistic religion that forms the foundation for Western ideals and values. In this case, general morality results in a specifically ordered social habitat.

As a result of the inductive influence of Taoism, Buddhism, and Chinese folk religion, much of Chinese culture and medicine turns on the belief that reality is the expression of the interplay of two opposing forces, commonly known as yin and yang. These are complementary rather than opposing forces since one cannot exist without the other. They exist naturally and neither can exist in isolation.

In the inductive world view, in other words, progress is less a function of linear and incremental progression and more a function of achieving equilibrium. For every yin there is a yang; for every pro there is a con. Neither can be eliminated. They must coexist, creating an optimal and desired state through balance and equipoise.

Such balance, however, is not the equivalent of the center of balance on the teeter-totter you might find at a children's playground. It is the center of balance you would find at the center of a circle or sphere. That center is truth, and the sphere encompassing it is the context within which it exists and by which it is defined.

Think of a tree. It has form and shape. It is tangible. We can touch it. But it exists in a broader context of weather, soil, and atmospheric conditions that are not the tree, but which help to define and shape it.

And so it is with life and business. Personal fulfillment and business success are not linear. They are not achieved through singular achievement. They are achieved only through the serenity and fulfillment of optimized equilibrium found at the center of context that defines our life.

Two

The False Dilemma Fallacy

Physicists deal with the science of the natural world. They can readily explain, for example, the mathematical laws behind a game of pool. Or the forces in play when a car travels down the highway.

Philosophers are the physicists of the world beyond the natural. They deal with issues such as existence, reason, and values.

Not that long ago there was considerable overlap between the two fields. Newton's *Philosophiæ Naturalis Principia Mathematica*, first published in 1687, set the stage for the emerging science of physics despite the reference to philosophy in its title.

While the literal translation of the original Latin word for philosophy is "the love of knowledge," generally accepted for much of history to mean any and all knowledge, most people today compartmentalize the two disciplines. Philosophy, a scientist would suggest, has little to contribute to science because its knowledge is not generally validated through scientific study and peer review.

This distinction is clearly evident in the modern world of business, although the language is different. Businesspeople distinguish between the objective and the subjective—the facts, typically defined by data, and the supposition, typically defined by conjecture or gut instinct.

It is, in fact, the Western distinction between philosophy and science, a gulf that has been expanding rapidly in the last three to four decades, that is at the heart of what ails much of corporate America today. The slide began the minute someone suggested that there could be such a thing as management science. When business schools and management consultants began to market the idea that successful business management could be modeled and graphed, corporate America lost more than its old habits. It lost its equilibrium. And with that, the long stumble began.

The problem is that philosophy and science have come to represent a false dilemma, sometimes called an either/or fallacy. A false dilemma is an informal fallacy in which it is falsely claimed that there are only a limited number of mutually exclusive options available to choose from.

There is, in fact, nothing mutually exclusive about science and philosophy. And there are, of course, plenty of additional ways to explain and explore reality. There is art, music, drama, dance, and a plethora of religions, superstitions, and supernatural belief systems to choose from.

Another false dilemma exists between deductive and inductive logic. And this is where the imbalance occurs in most companies today. Deductive and inductive logic are both powerful forms of reason. Like yin and yang, they are complementary forms of reason that facilitate the discovery of truth—and, in the case of business, success—when they are in balance.

When we begin to believe, as most businesspeople now do, that we can isolate analysis and instinct, fact and conjecture, and observation and speculation, we set the stage for failure. And it is almost guaranteed when we try to isolate and ignore the tools of inductive reason.

Consider these common statements, each uttered daily in C-suites across America:

The boss:

- "You are either on the team or you are not."

Rallying the troops:

- "There are winners, and there are losers."

The HR director:

- "We must grade performance to the bell curve. We can't have all fives. We must have some average employees and some who need improvement."

The motivational speaker:

- "Excuses are for losers."

Each is a form of the false dilemma fallacy. Each implies that truth is digital. It's not. It's not even close. In life and business, reality falls along a continuum of possibilities. And when you get to one end of the continuum, it's often a short step to back where you started.

False dilemmas don't have to be limited to two options, of course. There are trilemmas, quadrilemmas, and so on. Whenever reality can't be discreetly defined and doesn't lend itself to multiple choices or assignment to neat little geometric compartments in a two-dimensional box, a fallacy exists.

Can individual performance really be measured with any fairness and accuracy on a 1–5 scale? Can an employee's future potential really be objectively positioned in a "nine-box"? Can the progress on key strategic initiatives really be monitored using red, yellow, and green circles? Can a dashboard of metrics really tell you anything about how well a department, plant, or company is doing, or even what things may need attention?

In these cases, objectivity is a fallacy. No two people are alike. Performance is impacted by a plethora of external factors and influences that far outweigh personal effort and skill. The dashboard of your car tells you little about how well you are driving or whether a fatal accident waits around the next bend.

Why does business worship at the altar of deductive reason, often snuffing out any attempt to introduce inductive logic to problem-solving or strategic planning? Like most questions in life and business, there is no single, discreet answer.

The most obvious explanation is that our business schools, our consultants, and the business publishing industry all have a vested interest in promoting the fallacy. If business cannot be deductively analyzed and mapped, it cannot be taught, and consultants would have far less to share with their clients.

Technology, of course, also plays a role. It is difficult to explicitly build intuition into an Excel spreadsheet. And how would you chart a gut feeling or effectively communicate a hunch to your colleagues?

The world of technology that business currently lives in is a digital world ultimately defined in zeroes and ones. Artificial intelligence may ultimately change things, but today's technology is generally hostile to inductive reason because it can't be easily codified.

Investor activism and the growing influence of Wall Street on corporate America contribute to the bias. If you have ever listened in on a public corporation's quarterly earnings call, you know it's all about the x's and o's. The CFO and the CAO typically do much of the talking. No one wants to hear from the philosopher-in-residence.

Current trends in executive compensation exaggerate the proclivity. As compensation committees increasingly rely on equity compensation to influence executive behavior, the occupants of the C-suite increasingly recast themselves as accountants and financial analysts in an understandable effort to satisfy the incentives purposefully put in place to influence their behavior.

In the end, deductive logic is both seductive and addictive. It is the logic of the technology that has disrupted our commerce and redefined how we communicate and socialize. It is the logic aspiring executives are taught in business school. It is the language of Wall Street and the venture capitalists of Silicon Valley.

In theory it is the language of objectivity. It is the language of modern management science and the quest to manage our enterprises through the use of analytical tools and financial models designed to squeeze emotion, conjecture, and the anchor of experience out of the decision-making process. It is, in short, the language of change in which new companies emerge and old companies die off in the blink of an eye.

It is, however, a siren's song. If science is the standard, it is not an infallible one. Scientists continue to disprove the findings of other scientists with great frequency. The Martian canals first observed in 1877 by Italian astronomer Giovanni Schiaparelli were later found to be an optical illusion. The belief that the movement of the continents is explained by the Earth's expansion has been conclusively debunked. Even Einstein's static universe model was disproven by Edwin Hubble's discovery that the universe is expanding.

None of which is to say that deductive logic is predestined to be wrong. It is merely incomplete. It exists in context and should not be pursued in complete isolation.

Every yin has its yang. Every pro has a con. And the other side of the deductive-centric business model is the loss of equilibrium and a decline in the inductive influence of common sense, instinct, and experience. The resulting loss of rational equilibrium, in turn, leads to policies and processes that are, at best, misguided. Often, in fact, they are counterproductive.

Businesspeople need to take a page from Buddhism, at the heart of which is the concept of *emptiness*. As used by Buddhists, emptiness is not a synonym for nothingness. It denotes, instead, the lack of independent existence. Everything, in the Buddhist view, is interconnected and interdependent.

Traditional Chinese Medicine (TCM), some aspects of which are increasingly embraced by the Western medical community, takes the concept once step further. The practice of TCM is all about restoring the flow of *qi*—the force of life—through the correction of imbalance between qi's yin and yang components. This is the objective of all acupuncture, including cupping, the acupuncture therapy popularized by Michael Phelps at the 2016 Summer Olympics.

Think Yoda and Darth Vader in *Star Wars*. Both gain their power by channeling qi, the yin and yang essence of both "the Force" and "the Dark Side." It is the conflict between these two forces that gives the story entertainment value. Was the equilibrium to be completely destroyed by one finally finishing off the other, that value would evaporate.

But the conflict between deduction and induction in boardrooms across the West is not a battle between good and evil. The two, in fact, as the Tài jí tú symbol depicts, intertwine along a significant common border.

The key to business and career success is to live at the point of balance and to avoid the false dilemma fallacy that beckons from the extremes.

Three

The Supremacy of Process

Cause and effect. Businesses are built on the idea that certain values and behaviors will lead to sustainable profits. And that these same behaviors, if applied with consistency, will minimize risk to the company's financial health and stability.

At the heart of nearly every Western business practice is the firm belief that for every cause there is a predefined and predictable effect. And that every effect can be explained by root cause.

The standard operating procedure (SOP), one of the core tools of lean, is an excellent example. If you can determine root cause, the thinking goes, you can codify the process by which you can consistently achieve the desired outcome.

Computerized information systems have pushed the concept to near-religion status, largely out of necessity. A computer is digital in the most literal sense. If a process cannot be codified, a computer cannot facilitate or enforce it. And since computer-enabled processes can be a great source of productivity and risk avoidance, nearly all companies err on the side of codification even if flexibility must be sacrificed in order to achieve it.

The result is that process inevitably becomes the primary tool of business management. In addition to spending untold sums of money developing their processes, a great deal of corporate infrastructure is devoted to ensuring that those processes are followed to the letter.

Employees at all levels quickly learn that even if they achieve the desired result, their careers may be compromised if they are perceived to ignore established processes in doing so.

Casinos take process to the extreme. They start with the assumption that every dealer is a potential thief and layer process upon process to ensure that doesn't happen. They then layer on an elaborate hierarchy of oversight to make sure that the processes haven't broken down.

Based on my own personal experience working with dozens of companies, I would go so far as to say that process is the number one priority of *every* company today. It's not even a close contest. Forget about the common, but hollow, refrain that "Employees are our greatest asset" or "We put the customer first." It's BS.

In crime dramas it is often said, "Follow the money." And since time is money in the world of business, we can expand the advice to "Follow the time and money."

Map the time and money in any business today, and it will inevitably lead to process. Companies spend the vast majority of their time and resources today defining and enforcing processes. The customers, the employees, the culture, and the future are all distant laggards in the race for corporate attention.

Anyone who has worked in a company with more than one business unit knows that there is always tension between the corporate staff at headquarters and the geographically scattered business units. And I've worked on both sides of the table. Believe me, that tension is no fun for anyone.

In one of my roles as a business unit manager, I worked for a company that loved metrics. There was one metric that I followed more closely than any other, however, and I was the only one in this global company that even knew it existed. It was the number of organizational announcements that came out of corporate HR over a given period of time.

A new corporate position or a new occupant of an existing position could only mean one thing: I would soon have new processes that my team and I had to both power and accommodate. When a new corporate position is created, the occupant of that position is not going to sit on his or her hands all day. They want to get ahead just like everyone else. And for that they need the people in a position of authority to recognize their contribution.

The same goes for people newly assigned to an existing position. In all of my years in management, I never once had an employee that I promoted to an existing position come to me six months later and say, "My predecessor did a bang-up job. I haven't changed anything. I'm just riding on her coattails."

It just doesn't happen.

The problem, of course, is that staff positions, corporate or divisional, are typically not in a position to do much of anything without the help of the people who actually perform whatever task they are attempting to manage. They need processes to exert their influence. And they need information to develop and justify those processes.

To be clear, processes are not inherently bad. Every organization needs some process, or it will have chaos and anarchy. The problem is what I have come to call the law of organizational process. Process begets process. If one is good, ten are better. And a process is inherently designed to self-propagate. They grow. They get bigger. And the bigger they get, the harder they are to control—and harder yet to eliminate.

That's a bit misleading, of course. Processes are inanimate. They don't propagate themselves. It's the people who are charged with developing and managing the process that do that.

Sigmund Freud believed that we are the hero in all of our dreams and the monster in all of our nightmares. It's true. We are all self-absorbed. There are only degrees of selflessness. Even Mother Theresa, a true paragon of selflessness, believed that selflessness would benefit her in the long run. That's not to take anything away from her noble and caring character. It is merely to say, as I will repeat throughout this book, that nothing exists in isolation. Life is about context. For every yin there is a yang.

The yang of the business process is bureaucracy, inflexibility, excessive costs, and a culture that breeds resentment and disillusionment. Employees become the proverbial cogs on the gear. The human capital that every company needs to prosper is burnt out, disenfranchised, and short on enthusiasm. Results may be predictable and cost effective, but the team, as a whole, is stuck playing defense. There is no offense.

With our blind obsession with process, it should be no surprise to any business leader that many customers consider the entities from which they purchase goods and services to be inflexible and insensitive to the customer's needs. The employees, taught in much the same way that Pavlov taught his dogs, are stuck in the middle. Many inevitably fall back on process—the established policies—as a way to impersonalize the angst of the customer and defuse a negative situation. Of course, it seldom works.

And what do the companies do when the customer angst becomes palpable? Correct. They create more processes. In this case they develop customer satisfaction surveys—processes designed to measure the effectiveness of other processes—to measure customer satisfaction and reward or discipline their employees. And for the most part, these surveys are worthless, and worse.

I bought my first car in 1974. And I have hated the process ever since. I'd rather have surgery without anesthesia. It is a demeaning and frustrating experience with no upside. Sure, you get that new car smell, but that comes from the factory, not the dealer selling you the car.

The car companies finally got the message and have taken steps to make the buying process more customer-friendly. When you buy a car in the United States today, you will inevitably receive a follow-up customer survey asking you to rate your satisfaction with the experience. And the first question that inevitably comes to mind is, compared to what? A root canal?

And, once again, for every yin there is a yang; for every pro there is a con. In this case the efficiency of the delivery process is greatly diminished because the salesperson is now incentivized to spend time and effort on issues that the customer doesn't really care about. ("Do I really need to meet the service manager today? I don't need service right now; he won't remember me when I finally do, and I have a life.") And the customer is frustrated, of course, due to the additional time it takes the salesperson to follow the codified process for vehicle delivery and to coach the customer on what to say on the survey. ("Yes, I understand that your kids will starve if I don't give you the highest rating. Can I go now?")

The bottom line is that corporations are wasting a lot of money that could go into lowering the price or improving the product on processes to gauge customer satisfaction. And companies are dumb and happy, and possibly sowing the seeds of their destruction, because they believe they are doing a good job of customer service when, in fact, they are just annoying their customers.

The American Customer Satisfaction Index (ACSI), a national multi-industry measure of customer satisfaction developed by researchers at the University of Michigan in conjunction with the American Society for Quality and CFI Group, was 75.4 (0–100 Scale) for the third quarter of 2016. This was up from the trough of Q3 2015, following two years of steep decline, but below the peak achieved in 2013 and only modestly higher than the baseline developed in 1994.

This, of course, despite the fact that American companies have sunk billions of dollars over that twenty-two-year horizon educating, motivating, and equipping their employees to provide better customer service.

Employee engagement surveys are equally prolific and equally devoid of any real value. They represent a feeble attempt to again measure the effectiveness of a process with another process. In this case, however, the cost can be even greater if the process of measuring employee engagement increases disillusion instead. And it often does.

What are we thinking? A written or online survey can't possibly measure employee engagement in any meaningful way. And given the sensitivity of the subject, it is a slippery slope indeed. Is the survey truly anonymous? Will management sincerely follow up on the results? And how will I know if they do? Preexisting perceptions among employees will likely be exaggerated, for good or bad, without materially impacting the answers provided and giving management the feedback it hopes to get.

The cost of this obsession with process and the process of process? The IT budget is just the tip of the iceberg. That does not recognize the lost revenue that may result from the customer's sense that your company is difficult to do business with. Nor does it begin to measure the impact of covertly disgruntled employees.

The biggest cost component of process, however, is the cost of the organization necessary to manage it and enforce it. This is the part of the organization that adds no direct value to the creation, sale, and delivery of the product or service. And in most organizations, it is significant.

Why don't companies recognize this? There are two reasons.

The first is the mirage of objectivity that is rationalization. Anything can be rationalized. A clever and articulate individual can effectively argue any side of an issue and claim it to be the truth. Politicians do it every day. It all comes down to our willingness to share that argument. If we are predisposed to agree because we share a world view that is aligned with the rationalization, we admire the person making the argument, we are dependent on the person making the argument for our career advancement, or the argument has pushed the right emotional buttons, the hurdle to accepted truth can be very low indeed.

The tendency toward false rationalization, of course, is greatly enhanced by the fact that as you go further up the chain of command, the more uniformity there is in the world view of the individuals who occupy those roles. There are few true contrarians or mavericks in the ranks of corporate America today. Despite all the talk of diversity, there is remarkably little. Race and gender are the tip of the iceberg. There is even less diversity in management ranks when it comes to the way people interpret, process, and apply the lessons of the world around them.

The opportunity to rationalize false interpretations of reality is further enhanced by the imprecise nature of language. One might even say that language is the very essence of all rationalization, including false rationalization.

Language is strictly a man-made protocol designed to enhance the effectiveness of communication. It is not naturally occurring in the sense that oxygen and sunshine are. Humankind invented language to facilitate understanding.

But therein lies its Achilles' heel. In order to facilitate efficiency in communication, it must, by definition, be imprecise. It must be open to interpretation. And with interpretation comes the opportunity for abuse.

The best example of the abuse of lingual imprecision is the weasel words that have come to dominate our corporate and political dialogue. A term coined by author Steward Chaplin in 1900, and popularized by Theodore Roosevelt, these are the words and phrases that suck the meaning out of claims, much like the weasel sucks out the meat of the egg while leaving the shell intact. By compromising the context within which a claim is made, they provide cover for those who wish to mislead or misinform without being blatant about it.

Read any corporate-earnings release, and you'll find a bounty of examples. *"Essentially in line with previous guidance"* really means "We didn't do what we committed to, but we previously hedged our bet, and we're calling in the hedge." *"Adjusted EBITDA"* means "Our earnings weren't very good, but we're going to obscure that fact with adjustments that don't meet generally accepted accounting principles." *"We faced historically unprecedented headwinds"* means "We didn't do great, but it wasn't our fault."

If weasel words aren't enough, we can make up new words or use existing words in new ways that sound smart and sexy but don't really add any additional meaning. Instead of competing in markets, for example, we now occupy spaces. Those markets now have tails, which makes them sound awfully cute and cuddly, and the boss is data-centric, which is meant to imply the he or she is immune to bad judgment and whimsy.

The use of excessive jargon can be rationalized as a sign of linguistic progress, of course. But there is scant evidence that our corporate communication has gotten any more efficient as a result. If anything, I suspect, the average employee would suggest that the efficiency of our corporate communication has actually deteriorated over time.

Cost, of course, often goes hand in hand with inefficiency and inflexibility, and the cost of process is no exception. Beyond the sales impact of poor customer service and the tepid performance results of employees who are just going through the motions, process is often an impediment to innovation.

Innovation is essential to the long-term health of any company. And no company is knowingly inhibiting innovation. Many companies, however, undermine innovation through the restraining hand of their processes for managing costs and people.

Perhaps the most damaging process of all, however, is the erroneously named process by which most companies now manage "talent." For most it is a fundamentally misguided attempt to codify behaviors that promote teamwork, employee "ownership," and creative problem solving. Inevitably, however, employees are forced into a singular pattern of behavior that robs the company of the benefit of diversity of thought and style and impedes both real collaboration and innovation.

Most current talent management systems, of course, are mere manifestations of the fundamental belief in cause and effect. These, the promoters of such contemporary human resource processes argue, are the causes (i.e., behaviors and values) that must be instilled to achieve a high-performance (i.e., desirable) organization (i.e., outcome).

I will devote a chapter to the topic later in the book. For now, suffice it to say that talent management, as currently practiced, is a misguided attempt to deduce and codify human behavior and motivation. (i.e., create a process)

Not everything in business or life, however, can be deduced. The processes by which businesses deduce inevitably create false dilemma fallacies. The codification necessary to define predictable and repeatable processes creates, by its very nature, the fallacious argument that things like customer satisfaction and employee engagement are measurable in discrete terms.

In reality, processes help to define trail markers at best. They can help to inform. When they take on a life of their own, however, we are empowering them with an authority they are ill prepared to wield effectively.

Four

The Sine Wave

Two of the most prominent and important areas of study in the world of physics are the natural laws relating to flow and waves. Both have direct application to the world of business.

Almost everything in the natural world is flowing. The universe is expanding, and that expansion is accelerating. Water flows. Sound and light both flow. Blood, the very essence of life, flows. The degradation of matter and energy known as entropy, one of the most basic laws of the natural world, is a form of flow. The timeline of life itself, from conception to birth to death, flows like a raging river.

The most common form of flow in the universe, moreover, is the sine wave or sinusoid. It is the mathematical graph of the trigonometric function sine, a smooth and repetitive oscillation that is everywhere in the natural world. Sound, light, and other forms of electromagnetism flow in sine waves, as do the waves of the ocean, drifting snow, and the dunes of the desert.

The concepts of flow and sinusoids apply to business in a variety of ways. The economy operates in cycles. Machines cycle. We cycle count inventory to determine the accuracy of our records. The financial calendar cycles. Customers order in cycles. We even have a cyclical sector of the stock market.

Most Western companies and their shareholders loathe the natural rhythm of cycles, particularly when it comes to financial performance.

They want the company's financial performance to improve *every* quarter, no excuses. "Cycles are for wimps."

Like most absolute statements, of course, there is a whiff of truth to that perspective. As Henry Ford said, "If you think you can do a thing or think you can't do a thing, you're right." Sheer determination counts for a lot.

By failing to acknowledge the fundamental law of cycles, however, we often do more harm than good. We exaggerate the amplitude of the wave. That's great on the upside but can be deadly on the downside.

A Japanese business executive and good friend said it best: "American companies like to exceed the financial forecast by as much as possible. 'Sales in my region are 30 percent over plan,' is a source of great pride. But that's not the right perspective. If your sales exceed plan by such an amount you are either a poor planner and have likely missed even more opportunities, or there is an anomaly in your market. Next year, of course, you will try to increase sales even further. By then, however, the anomaly may no longer exist. As a result you will make bad decisions in an effort to beat a standard that wasn't real to begin with."

When it comes to corporate performance, the ascending straight line is deductively attractive for obvious reasons. It appeals to the hero complex in all of us and reinforces the reassuring but naïve notion that we alone are in control of our destiny.

The sinusoid wave, on the other hand, is yin and yang in motion. It is induction over time. If you attach the end of a pencil to the center of a circle with the sharpened end facing out and you rotate the pencil 360 degrees while moving it from left to right at a steady pace to introduce the element of time, you will draw the sinusoid wave that shapes light, sound, and a host of other phenomenon in pure and applied mathematics, physics, and engineering.

By refusing to acknowledge the natural law of the sinusoidal wave, we may elongate the wavelength, but we will not eliminate the natural rhythm of the universe. It will ultimately catch up to us and by denying it a company often spawns a self-destructive culture of misappropriated energy and deceit that ultimately enhances the negative amplitude of the next trough.

Three candidates are interviewing for an accounting job at a large, multinational company. The interviewer asks the first candidate, "What is two plus two?"

"Four," comes the confident response.

The interviewer then asks the second candidate, "What is two plus two?"

"Five," comes the timid response.

On to the third candidate, "What is two plus two?"

"What do you want it to be?"

"You've got the job!"

Thankfully, there are few companies that take the deceit to that level. But there is a reason the Securities and Exchange Commission puts so much regulatory effort into period accounting. And many companies will jettison employees or cut fringes and benefits, directly impacting the quality of life of their employees, in response to what may be the natural rhythm of the business.

That's not always the case, of course. Sometimes painful choices are necessary for the long-term survival of the business due to fundamental shifts in the market. The key, of course, is discerning which is which. When are such measures truly necessary and when are they merely destructive tricks to maintain the stock price at any cost?

Perhaps the most valuable lesson businesspeople can take from the world of physics is the propensity for processes and practices to overshoot the mark and perpetuate themselves beyond need or relevance in much the same way sine waves exhibit positive and negative amplitudes above and below the center line.

Peter F. Drucker noted that, "If you want to do something new you have to stop doing something old." Most executives, however, fail miserably at this task. New processes are prolifically generated, but old processes seldom die. They just live on, consuming valuable resources, including management time and attention, and supporting bad decisions.

The reason goes back to Sir Isaac Newton and the laws of motion, specifically the concept of momentum. A ball thrown through the air has momentum. A truck driving down the highway has momentum. Even a process has momentum.

Business processes are developed when a need is perceived. A manifestation of the deductive belief in the supremacy of cause and effect, a process is an attempt to codify behaviors to achieve a desired result or to preclude an unattractive one.

The problem is that processes inevitably take on a life of their own. They gain momentum. Processes are designed and administered by people, and people, as Sigmund Freud reminded us, are always motivated by self-interest. People have pride of authorship, the desire to compete effectively with their peers for reward and advancement in an ever-narrowing hierarchy, and, of course, an instinct for self-preservation.

A process won't be terminated, therefore, when the returns it generates have exceeded the investment required to maintain it, it distracts from other processes that may contribute more value, or it is no longer relevant to the current state. Eventually, however, it will hit bottom—the trough of the sine curve, if you will. And, by necessity, it will be revised or eliminated.

By then, however, it may be too late. Others may be called upon to do what the owners of the process did not do. Or the business may have to enter a period of painful recovery. Either way, the optimal results will not be achieved.

This reality is clearly recognized by the increasingly common business mantra, "If it ain't broke, break it." Once a process reaches the middle or centerline of its return, it appears to remain productive and advisable, although that is about to change. It is here, in the sweet spot, where change should optimally take place.

This is the point of equilibrium, the center of balance between yin and yang, productivity and waste, return and loss. It is here that all business should seek to reside, in a position of balance between data and instinct, between expectation and experience, between great innovation and folly.

Five

Connection

A braham Maslow (1908–1970) was an American psychologist best known for the development of Maslow's hierarchy of needs. It postulates that humans cannot achieve self-esteem or self-actualization—the fulfillment of one's potential—until they first have food to eat, have a safe place to stay, and have established connection with the world around them.

The first two needs are pretty obvious. Unfortunately, poverty and homelessness have not been eradicated despite the unprecedented accumulation of wealth that has occurred in the developed world.

Regarding the innate need for connection, it is well documented that Americans feel increasingly isolated and lonely. A quarter of us live alone. Our families are smaller and more geographically dispersed. Our lifestyles are increasingly compromised by our quest to feed and shelter ourselves, and the social institutions that previously brought us together in safe and nonthreatening environments are in decline. Suicide rates continue to rise.

Contrary to popular myth, social media has not bridged the gulf. Social media is a platform for social entertainment, not real connection. And to the extent that the time spent online reduces the time we connect face-to-face, it may actually be contributing to the increasing sense of isolation.

Early in my career I had the chance to meet Lawrence A. Appley (1904–1997), who served as president of the American Management

Association (AMA) from 1948 to 1968 and chairman from 1968 to 1974. He was the chairman emeritus of the AMA and serving on the board of directors of the company I worked for when our paths crossed.

Mr. Appley, according to legend, did not have a desk in his office. And he obviously had, during those years, neither a smart phone, a tablet, or a personal computer. He had no access to social media or the Internet.

He believed in face-to-face communication, pure and simple. And he was not alone among that generation of business leaders. While they may be more frequently remembered for the extended lunch and the time they spent on the golf course, they actively pursued activities that fed personal connection.

When I first became the president of a public company, I, too, indulged in a game of golf with the lead bankers that supported our business. As a mentor once advised me, when you need the support of your banker most is not the time for starting a relationship.

Today, of course, the relationship would undoubtedly be moot. I'm sure the latitude for lending decisions made by the lending officers of the big banks who currently control corporate lending is greatly constricted by risk assessment boards and inviolate financial processes.

The sense of isolation, however, is not limited to the C-suite. The results of Gallup's annual *State of the American Workplace* survey, issued in February 2017, found that a full 70 percent of American workers are not engaged at work. That is both alarming and telling considering the amount of time, effort, and money most companies have spent over the last decade attempting to personalize the work environment in order to boost productivity, collaboration, and loyalty.

Workplaces are increasingly open and comfortable. Common areas now boast Ping-Pong tables for play and beanbags and isolation pods for relaxation and ideation. The food is better, the atmosphere is cheery, and more attention has been paid to outdoor spaces where employees can sit in a park or walk around a small lake. (When they aren't being worked to death.)

So why are more than two-thirds of American workers disengaged?

The reason is pure Maslow. Many Americans today have a deep, unfulfilled yearning for connection that even they may be unaware of. Angst is merely the transference.

Modern concepts of management are compounding the problem. Perhaps chief among them is the largely misguided notion of brutal honesty and transparency in the employer-employee relationship. Managers and supervisors are incessantly instructed to be direct in their job performance evaluations and that, by definition, some portion of the organization must be underperforming relative to the whole.

Many companies, as a result, force employee performance reviews into a bell curve distribution, justifying the move to employees by attempting to convince them that a rating of 2 on a scale of 5 is not a "bad" thing. It is, instead, a kind of gift to the employee built on a noble foundation of transparency and a sincere desire to help employees improve and realize their true potential. It's a lie.

As Scott Adams wrote in *The Dilbert Principle*, "In theory, the Performance Review process can be thought of as a positive interaction between a 'coach' and an employee, working together to achieve maximum performance. In reality, it's more like finding a dead squirrel in your backyard and realizing the best solution is to fling it onto your neighbor's roof. Then your obnoxious neighbor takes it off the roof and flings it back, as if he had the right to do that. Ultimately, nobody's happy, least of all the squirrel."

You probably turned out to be a pretty good person. Not perfect, perhaps, but you have your strengths. And how did you get those strengths? Did your parents conduct annual performance reviews wherein they detailed all of your flaws? And did they rate you and your siblings on a bell curve? Or did you follow their example or otherwise find the chance to develop under their protective wing?

In reality, many companies today have not only broken the implied contract between employer and employee that helped shape the American century in post–World War II America, they actively cull what they believe to be the worst performing segment of the employee population.

Popularized by General Electric and others, the practice is conceptually attractive at some level. By culling the poorest performers and replacing them with workers expected to perform at the highest level, in theory, the aggregate performance of the team can be steadily upgraded over time.

As Yogi Berra once observed, however, "In theory there is no difference between theory and practice. In practice there is." Seldom does evaluating performance to some predefined distribution produce a higher level of aggregate performance. Quite the opposite is generally true.

The reasons are simple and straightforward. The concept is built on an assumption that personal performance is knowable and measurable and the conviction that the hiring and advancement processes are truly objective. Both assumptions often prove false in practice.

Unfortunately, these policies are not impact-neutral. They are not just misguided, they are destructive. Both serve to undermine the sense of connection that is so essential to human fulfillment. Both serve not to drive productivity but to suppress it through alienation.

If companies wish to continually strive for excellence, they must first strive to provide employees with a sense of connection. Not with the company per se, but with each other, including management.

As noted throughout the book, however, people respond to what you inspect, not what you expect. Behavior trumps communication every time. If you say the right things but your behavior contradicts your words, no matter how sincerely they may be delivered, you are wasting your breath. People won't believe you. And the distrust won't even be performance-neutral. It will ultimately be counterproductive.

Trust, as discussed elsewhere in this book, is critical to connection. Not only does trust lower the barriers of connection, it actually promotes it. People want to be connected to people they trust. They will seek them out. Don't you?

So, while it is true that a company must actively manage its employees in the interest of performance, it is equally true that dehumanizing employees to the extent that relationships and connections are inhibited is counterproductive. Some balance between the recognition of our individual humanity and the need for collective performance must be struck.

Six

Marketing

Contemporary marketing, like so many other current business processes, has become increasingly deductive. Marketers don't so much brainstorm creative and original solutions as they deduce them by mining Big Data and other sources of information believed to be both objective and factual. In theory, this is progress.

Emphasis on theory. There is little hard evidence that contemporary marketing plans are any more consistently successful than those developed in the years before computers and the concept of quantitative marketing emerged.

Why? If there is a professional process for marketing, why can't everyone do it? Every company has access to the same texts, the same consultants, and the same data. If marketing can be truly professional—as in objective and calculating—why don't marketing professionals perform at the same consistent level as, say, airline pilots? If pilots performed at the same level as business executives, most of us would be dead.

The simple reason for the difference in performance is that the process of flying an airplane lends itself to codification. Airplanes respond to a very specific and inviolate set of natural laws of lift, propulsion, and aerodynamics. Pilots and their employers, air traffic controllers, and plane manufacturers alike understand these laws and have developed detailed and elaborate processes and check lists to insure safe travel.

The very idea of creative insight is, of course, much more difficult to define, much less codify. While the most successful marketing campaigns of the past often seem brilliant with the benefit of hindsight, many brazenly rejected conventional wisdom and the data that supported it at the time.

Likewise, some of the great marketers of their time might not have been so successful in a different time and place. Steve Jobs wasn't. As you may recall the board at Apple sidelined him in the middle of his career. He was ultimately reinstated and the magic returned, but his career did not follow a straight trajectory.

Our preoccupation with cause and effect, unfortunately, has bled the creativity and opportunity out of much of our contemporary marketing. Even if an idea can by justified "by the numbers," the opportunity may not be material given the simple fact that it has passed the codified test of return on investment (ROI). It's a process filled with bias, and most of the best ideas throughout history could not pass an ROI analysis before someone took the chance anyway and made history.

The first ATM, for example, was installed by Barclays Bank in north London in 1967—*fifty years ago.* In 1969 Chemical Bank installed the first ATM in the United States at its branch in Rockville Centre, New York. The idea took decades to catch on, however. Now ubiquitous around the globe, bank marketers at the time of the ATM's invention refused to believe that customers would conduct personal financial business with a machine.

And while Apple is most commonly associated with development of the graphical user interface (GUI) and mouse now used by virtually every PC under the sun, Xerox had conceived of the GUI in 1972, years before Apple would introduce the legendary Macintosh. Steve Jobs would see the GUI and mouse during a sanctioned tour of Xerox's Palo Alto Research Center (PARC) in 1979. No one suggests he stole the technology. (Some accounts suggest that Apple was already working on a GUI of its own.) All those present at the meeting do agree, however, that Jobs became quite animated in his disbelief that Xerox was not applying the technology commercially. Jobs saw the potential. He didn't model it. Xerox probably did. And it vacated the PC market, a market that Jobs apparently believed Xerox could have owned.

The problem is that there is, by definition, no data from the future. All data exists in the past or current tense. Building all of your marketing plans on data alone is like driving your car by looking only at the rearview mirror.

You can, of course, model the future. And you might even use current and past data to extrapolate trends and thus improve the accuracy of your projection. At its best, however, modeling is an inexact science and its effectiveness can only be truly known after the fact, when its value has greatly diminished.

The root problem with quantitative marketing, however, is that buying decisions are driven by personal motivations, and those motivations typically result from Freudian self-interest. As a result, data often quantifies the result, not the root cause. Marketing, on the other hand, is all about stimulating motivation.

We can measure resulting trends, but without the why behind the what, we probably can't predict a change in behavior with much accuracy. And the why behind existing trends, by definition, is probably being satisfied in existing ways. That's where the data that a modeled trend comes from. It is a reflection of existing reality.

That's great if you just want to understand existing reality, but generally not enough to launch a new product or marketing plan that is going to upend the existing market. For that you need to know how consumers *will* react, not how they have reacted in the past. The motivation may remain constant, but it may not. And the consumer, as Steve Jobs well understood, is not in a position to tell you they want something they don't realize is possible or will overturn their existing behavioral paradigm.

That is why I've never been a big fan of focus groups. The sample size is statistically small, there is always the issue of "anticipated expectations" that I write about in a later chapter, and people can't tell you what they don't currently know. A focus group might reveal a crumb of relevant and valuable information. But it might not. And there is always the potential to be misled. On balance, therefore, I believe caution is appropriate.

As I have previously argued, cultures can generally be categorized into those built on a foundation of deductive logic and those built on a foundation of inductive logic. Human behavior, by and large, can be classified in much the same way. But neither culture nor behavior is ever exclusively one or the other. And the classification is both variable and time sensitive.

When I go to a restaurant, my choice of what to order may be essentially deductive. I might have recently gone to the doctor, for example, and she advised me to lose some weight, so I order a salad, dressing on the side. A week from now, however, I walk to my table in the same restaurant and subconsciously note that several patrons are eating the same dish. My subconscious speculates that the dish must be good (it does not occur to me that the restaurant may have run out of everything else), and I, too, in very much a departure from my past behavior, order the same dish.

As a general rule, I believe the buying decisions made through inductive logic are going to be more profitable for the provider. Inductive logic, in general, results in stronger emotions. "Deduction be damned; this is what I want, and I'm willing to pay for it." Even the customer may not know why.

Brand identity is generally inductive. Aspirational brands are alluring because they provide an association that we find attractive. It's a reverse process to cause and effect. It's effect and cause, if you will.

If the consumption of your product or service is driven by deductive logic, on the other hand, the consumer is likely to be less attached to his or her decision. The market is also likely to be more competitive since everyone can decipher the deductive thought process in the same way you did.

Many commercial transactions are influenced by both types of logic, of course. If I am buying a house, I may have a very real and inviolate need for a certain number of bedrooms. But, as any experienced realtor will tell you, I will also be influenced by the home's "curb appeal."

Ask any ten realtors to define curb appeal, however, and you are likely to get up to ten different answers. In the end, it comes down to the same inductive logic employed by Associate Justice of the Supreme Court of the United States, Potter Stewart, who wrote a short opinion on the obscenity case, *Jacobellis v. Ohio* (1964), stating, "I know it [pornography] when I see it."

But if it can't be deduced, how do marketers tap into the lucrative vein of inductive logic? It all comes down to human behavior and the motivations that drive it. Which is why I believe marketers should spend as much time studying philosophy and psychology as they spend studying the hard science of statistical modeling.

Early in my career, I worked for a consumer-products company for which product design was critical. All of the products in the marketplace more or less shared the same functionality and a very comparable price. Buying decisions, therefore, were typically driven by appearance and brand.

And we had one designer who accounted for the vast majority of our most successful products. He was, in fact, a bit of a celebrity in our rather small industry.

As a result, we often sent him to trade shows in places like New York, Paris, and Frankfurt, Germany. And while he was a good ambassador for the company, he always took some time to walk the city and visit several local museums. I know because I signed his expense reports.

Unfortunately, his creative behavior—at company expense—was a bone of contention with others in the company. And I heard about it. He was alone, after all, in the freedom he was given on the company dime. And people resented it.

One day, as a result, I raised the topic with him. I just wanted to get his take. And he had one.

He explained that he was not entirely conscious of the source of his designs. He knew, however, that subconscious inspiration played a significant role. When he visited a museum, therefore, he gave no thought to the company or its products. He simply immersed himself in the subject matter of the museum.

At some future point in time, however, a design inevitably emerged from his subconscious, which he would then evaluate from a more objective marketing perspective. He rejected many of his own designs, but every once in a while, a keeper would emerge. He couldn't pinpoint the source, but he knew that it had somehow been stimulated by what he had experienced. No cause and effect, if you will—only inductive observation. (Needless to say, I ultimately encouraged him to visit more museums and to travel at will.)

Today, of course, every consumer-products company is trying to figure out how to market to the millennial generation. The future belongs to the young. Statistically, that makes sense. And since most people my age (I'm sixty-two) have at least some melancholy about lost youth, it's a poetic sentiment attractive to most business executives and creative professionals.

Many marketers are consequently preoccupied with the millennials. But I think marketers have always been preoccupied with the younger generation. They're just a lot more fun to market to. They are on the cusp of developing social trends and typically embrace the latest technology. (Ironically, the oldest generation has most of the wealth statistically.)

This is why every marketer today has a presence on social media. That's where the younger generations live, which, of course, is a lifestyle laden with both pros and cons, yins and yangs.

I believe, however, that there is a more fundamental truth about millennial behavior that I have yet to hear being discussed in the world of marketing and business. And it has to do with the sine wave theory of existence that I strongly subscribe to and discussed in chapter 4.

Generally speaking, the sine wave theory holds that the natural rhythm of life and the universe is a series of peaks and troughs, much like the waves of the ocean. Everything happens in a cycle.

Contemporary American culture, as I've argued throughout this book, is built on a foundation of deductive logic dating all the way back to Aristotle. As a result, as noted, we believe in the supremacy of cause and effect, the absolute nature of morality, individual rights and freedoms that may conflict with the collective good (e.g., the right to own guns of any kind), and the ability to personalize and defer to our institutions (e.g., the rule of law).

We have ridden that horse for a long time. And with the acceleration of change that has made the world smaller and has dramatically changed both the way we obtain information and communicate with each other, our journey along the linear path of deduction has accelerated.

And that, I believe, has resulted in a lot more angst and disillusionment. In the extreme, deduction implies that there is a reason for everything. This severely distorts our perceptions of personal accountability. If I fail, it is not my fault; I am a victim. If I succeed, on the other hand, I deserve to. I am good, maybe great.

Neither perspective is very healthy. The former leads to a sense that you are not in control. The latter contributes to personal isolation. You can't connect with people you feel superior to.

Stress and pressure are two different things. Pressure is a function of workload, the time available to perform the work, and the potential consequences of that work. Air traffic controllers, without a doubt, feel a lot of pressure.

Stress, however, results when we are asked to perform tasks we have little control over. As long as we feel we have the training, the tools, and the freedom to perform a task, most of us experience relatively little stress, even in high-pressure jobs. Survey after survey finds, however, that the majority of Americans experience moderate to severe stress in the workplace, and it is costing American companies billions in lost productivity and effectiveness.

The Chinese, in my experience living and working there, appear to suffer far less stress than the average American. Despite the frenetic pace of everyday life in China, where change is measured by the stopwatch, not the calendar, and the general lack of both privacy and personal space, the Chinese I met along the way appeared to move on far more easily than their Western counterparts in response to disappointment, denial, and loss. Even the wealthiest Chinese, who often wear their wealth on their sleeves, I sensed, would quickly rebound if they lost it all, in sharp contrast to the Western male who lost his prized sports car.

I attribute this difference to the fact that Chinese culture is built on a foundation of inductive logic. In the Buddhist and Tao tradition, everything is interconnected. Nothing exists in isolation. Good and bad fortune, therefore, aren't personal. They are simply what they are. There are no victims; there is only bad fortune. Nobody is truly superior to anyone else; some are simply luckier, although to the Chinese luck has more to do with fortune than the random spirit it is considered in the West.

Even culture, however, is subject to the universal force of the sine wave. The Chinese, based on my observation, are gradually becoming more deductive in their world view, although cultural change comes slowly in the Middle Kingdom. And American culture, I believe, will ultimately reach the end of its rope and will pivot toward induction. It will have to. People will find life to be so stressful and unfulfilling that they will have little choice but to adopt the "qué será será" world view.

The young inevitably drive cultural transformation, and the American millennials, I believe, will lead the way to a more inductive set of personal priorities. Marketers and employers (and politicians) are already feeling the winds of change. Millennials demand a better work-life balance and are generally open to acquiring far less "stuff" than their parents. They'll even share or do without things like cars or manicured lawns in the suburbs, which were essential to individual identity among my own generation.

During the 2016 election cycle, we thought of the millennial generation as political progressives. But categorizing voters by some perceived core ideology is a very deductive way to look at voting patterns. It belies a preoccupation with deduction that is at the heart of those generations that have defined the political landscape for the last half-century.

But I don't believe that millennials think in such prepackaged terms. I think they have seen both the great potential and the great weakness of extreme deductive logic that the members of my own generation have raised to a near-religion. Marketers and employers must adapt to this changing world view or face the inevitable flight of customers and employees.

Which is to say, simply put, that they have to turn around and head back toward the middle, to the center of balance between induction (the round peg) and deduction (the square hole). Don't tell; inspire. Don't demand; lead. Forget the principles of acquisition you learned in business school; focus on the principles of personal fulfillment, connection, and trust foremost among them.

Seven

Raison d'être

I hope we shall crush in its birth the aristocracy of our moneyed corporations, which dare already to challenge our government to a trial of strength and bid defiance to the laws of our country.

THOMAS JEFFERSON

The modern corporation can trace its roots back to the Middle Ages, when the British king formally recognized English towns as independent entities in the eyes of the law. The first commercial corporations were later chartered by the monarchy to further the economic interests of the crown. Queen Elizabeth, for example, chartered the British East India Company in 1600 to challenge the Dutch-Portuguese monopoly on the spice trade.

In time, the American colonies borrowed the idea. Colonial legislatures chartered corporations to build canals, bridges, and roads and to pursue other economic endeavors in the public interest. Each corporation was chartered for a specific purpose and for a specific period of time.

In a series of rulings rarely studied by school children, however, the US Supreme Court, starting with its 1819 ruling in *Trustees of Dartmouth College v. Woodward*, gradually chipped away at government control over the corporations the states chartered. The modern era of self-defined corporate purpose fully materialized with the 1886 US Supreme Court ruling in *Santa Clara County v. Southern Pacific Railroad*. Invoking the Fourteenth Amendment to the US Constitution—the "due process" amendment designed to protect emancipated slaves—the court ruled that a corporation is a "person," with all of the constitutional rights and protections, save voting, enjoyed by individuals.

This isn't surprising given the deductive logic on which American culture is built. The political system built on that culture emphasizes individual rights and personal freedoms. Our political institutions, such as the rule of law and the democratic election, are specifically designed to protect those rights in the service of the common good.

It is entirely logical, therefore, that Americans have come to embrace the institution at a very personal level. Institutions like the rule of law, our military, and the right to free speech and assembly are symbols of those rights and freedoms, and we embrace them accordingly.

The extension goes both ways, however, and over time we have come to view ourselves, in part, as an extension of our favorite institutions. We draw identity from them. Whether it's the National Rifle Association, Mothers Against Drunk Driving, the National Audubon Society, the National Organization of Women, or Shriners International, we identify at a very personal level with the institutions that we support. We buy their tote bags and put their bumper stickers on our cars. (A social phenomenon I have yet to see anywhere else in the world.)

Years after graduation many people continue to personalize the college or university they attended. And why are we so consumed with spectator sports? A sports team is an institution. Yet we personalize them in the extreme. We cheer their successes and mourn their losses. We emblazon our homes and our clothing with their logos and colors. We spend material amounts of our leisure time following their fortunes.

Social media and the Internet have contributed greatly to the humanization of our institutions. YouTube experts and entertainers, bloggers, and Tweeters with a large following have essentially risen to the level of an institution. In return, we "follow" their institution and share our judgment publicly with our digital "thumb," adding, in the process, to our own personal identity and sense of self.

Social media, as a result, has contributed greatly to the compartmentalization of Western society and the isolation of its members. We exist in packs, both constructive and destructive, in the most literal sense.

These associations, however, are strictly two-dimensional and don't fulfill the need for connection that Maslow referred to. They are hollow and superficial and do little to allay a decaying sense of personal relevance.

Most companies, of course, have come to embrace social media as a platform for influencing consumer behavior. They want to interact with their consumers, or potential consumers, by creating a sense of institutional community and reaping the rewards of loyalty they believe will follow.

Many netizens fear, in fact, that corporations are taking over the Internet. And they are. They follow your every move; they know your buying habits; and they are financially compromising the bloggers, opinion shapers, and others in an attempt to encourage them to promote the company narrative.

Even the news has been compromised. Newspapers and magazines have always run ads, of course. Now, however, many major online news sites mix real news and "sponsored" content on the same page, making minimal effort to differentiate one from the other.

The corporate social media community is a false community, however, a Potemkin village designed to personalize the institution in the interest of commerce. It is a ruse, akin to the attempt by Western monarchies of the past to use missionaries to promote their political agenda in developing countries such as China and most of the former colonies of the leading European powers.

While corporations are actively promoting an image of social responsibility, relatively few corporations in America today embrace social responsibility where the rubber meets the road. (There are exceptions, to be sure.) The former CEO of General Electric, Jack Welch, summed up the typical American boardroom perspective when he wrote, "...a CEO's primary social responsibility is to assure the financial success of the company."

Even those who have been enriched by today's corporations seldom feel the sense of civic duty collectively shared by the business magnates and industrialists who dominated the economy at the close of the nineteenth century. Men like John D. Rockefeller, J. P. Morgan, Andrew Carnegie, and Henry Ford acquired immense fortunes but also made lasting investments in their communities.

Men like Warren Buffett, Bill Gates, and Mike Ilitch, the founder of Little Caesars pizza, continue the legacy of philanthropy, but they no longer represent the norm of their wealthy peers. Instead of living in mixed neighborhoods, albeit in the biggest house, many of today's wealthiest businesspeople use the money to escape to their gated communities, the hills of Tuscany, or their private islands—optics be damned.

Corporate citizenship is a classic case of wanting to eat your cake and keep it too. If corporations want the rights of individual citizens, they must take on the obligations of citizenship in an advanced, progressive society. They, like the members of any community, must be judged by their contribution to that community.

Paying taxes and providing employment are not enough, just as it is not enough for parents to simply provide food and shelter to their children. As Maslow noted, that won't even get them half way to the universal goal of personal fulfillment.

In many Eastern cultures, in contrast to the institutional West, all relationships are personal relationships. Largely due to the inductive foundation of their world view, they have a difficult time viewing an institution through the same lens that they view family and friends.

Which is why driving in China is one of life's more harrowing experiences. China has the same traffic laws that the most developed Western countries do. But they are routinely ignored by virtually everyone. The rule of law, after all, is merely an institution. To the inductive mind you have no more obligation to a traffic law than you do to any other institution.

Neither extreme, in my opinion, is appropriate. Companies have to make money to survive. And it is certainly true that a financially successful company will provide far better opportunities and job security to its employees than one that is struggling to pay its bills.

The key, yet again, is balance. While a business must be allowed to make money, it must assume some social responsibility if it is to assume the rights of citizenship. That, in fact, is essential in the age of social media when the lines between the individual and the institution are increasingly blurred. Our institutions, if unchecked, will otherwise overpower the individual, further isolating one person from another and dehumanizing our society and culture.

It's already happening.

Eight

Diversity

Every corporate executive today talks about the importance of diversity. Few corporations, however, achieve it.

According to the *Missing Pieces Report: The 2016 Board Diversity Census of Women and Minorities on Fortune 500 Boards*, published by Alliance for Board Diversity in collaboration with Deloitte, women and minorities occupy only 30.8 percent of the board seats among Fortune 500 companies. And according to research published by *Fortune* in 2014, only 4 percent of the CEOs of the Fortune 500 were minorities, while 5 percent were women.

Why? At a time when women make up close to half of the entire workforce of Fortune 500 companies, why aren't they and minorities scaling the corporate ladder to its upper rungs?

Part of the explanation, of course, can be blamed on lingering but persistent gender and racial discrimination. I suggest, however, that there is another form of discrimination that must shoulder much of the blame. Its harmful effects may not rise to the level of social injustice perpetrated by gender and racial discrimination, but the impact on corporate performance is profound nonetheless.

The fact is that if you look at the 70 percent of the Fortune 500 board seats occupied by Caucasian males you will note a remarkable similarity between the occupants. They are all cut from the same cloth. Many were educated in the same small basket of elite schools. Nearly all share the same world view. And most share remarkably similar political and economic values.

The simple reason for this homogeneity is that it is natural for people to want to associate with people who share their world view and general outlook. New board members are typically selected by the existing board. Yes, they must ultimately be ratified by the shareholders, but few nominees are ever turned away once the process gets to that point.

Having served on the board of directors of four public companies, I can tell you from experience that most board members take their responsibilities quite seriously and actively look for new board members whose skills and experience complement those of the existing board members.

That said, however, there is an unwritten protocol on most boards that places a high value on new board members "fitting in." It is never discussed or even consciously acknowledged. But it is there. It is only human. And pragmatic, to a point. A board member who cannot get along with the rest of the board will ultimately contribute little more than angst and anxiety.

I once worked with a US company that was considering a joint venture with a Japanese company competing in a related market. The CEO was skeptical of the idea but was finally persuaded to fly to Japan to meet with his Japanese counterpart. On the plane ride home, he noted with some satisfaction and obvious surprise, "They're just like us." And the deal was ultimately consummated.

It is this form of discrimination, I believe, that is, in part, holding the ascension of women and minorities at bay in corporate America. Even among those Caucasian males who are not consciously or overtly misogynic or racist, these identity groups must nonetheless pass the litmus test of "fitting in." (Of course, this in itself can be racist or misogynist, but I think you can see my point.)

While gender and racial equality is important to the achievement of social justice, it is the diversity of world views that is critical to sound decision making in the arena of trade and commerce. That, in turn, will promote all other forms of diversity, including gender and race.

And what do I mean by that?

As largely deductive thinkers, Americans put great value on the direct linkage between cause and effect. Every cause leads to a pre-determined effect or outcome. Our decisions and our beliefs presuppose it.

We act, in other words, on our expectations. And these are either taught or acquired through past experience. If we make a decision to do X, we expect that Y will be the result because that is precisely what happened last time.

There is, however, a slight problem that is seldom acknowledged. Reality is not an absolute. The scientific method, the most deductive and seductive of all analytical processes, is a methodology for interpreting reality. It is not, of and by itself, a body of absolute knowledge. Most scientific discoveries, in fact, are ultimately proven to be in error.

Few decisions in life, much less business, are made with an abundance of data. Even the data we think we have is often incomplete, inaccurate, or misleading. It is often, in fact, supposition or conjecture parading as cold, hard facts.

Psychologists refer to this phenomenon as precognitive conclusion. Simply stated, we process only a small portion of the data our senses make available before reaching a conclusion. Some scientists believe we actually consider less than one-billionth of the facts available.

It's all a matter of efficiency. If we didn't reach conclusions precognitively, we would never get out of bed in the morning. We would spend all day processing what is, on most mornings, superfluous data.

The threshold for reaching a conclusion is different for all of us. Some of us process very little data. We literally jump to conclusions. Others require a great deal of data before forming a conclusion, often giving the impression of indecisiveness.

As a result of precognitive conclusion, we essentially see and hear what we expect to. Or, perhaps more accurately, what we allow ourselves to—our world view—since those expectations are defined by the bias of our past experience.

Our individual management style is likewise shaped by our past experience. Again, this can include actual real life experience and taught experience, assuming the teaching took hold.

At the social level, it is this diversity in world view that gives us culture and makes the world an interesting place. Without it we would be a community of androids.

In the organizational world, however, it is this diversity in world view that provides us with sound decision making. Problems must be analyzed from all perspectives. Picking from a basket of solutions will always lead to a better result than will the forced acceptance of a single solution.

The corporate landscape is littered with the corpses of companies whose board of directors stood by and watched them disintegrate. Where was the board of Enron when its executives were erecting Potamkin schemes that cost the shareholders and employees everything? Where was the board of AIG when it played a key role in driving the global economy into the worst crisis since the Great Depression? Where was the board of Kodak? Of Pan Am? The list goes on and on.

While I don't know any of the directors involved personally, I am quite confident that they were competent and conscientious in their roles. I suspect, however, that they all looked at each crisis through the same lens. As a result, they didn't see it coming and didn't act while they had the chance.

The same problems exist within the management ranks of most companies. In fact there may be less diversity there because of the inordinate amount of power held by the CEO and the reality that the people who make it into that corner office typically have a very low threshold of precognitive conclusion. Most are decidedly decisive. To an extent they have to be.

The process of talent management, of course, reinforces a similar one-dimensional profile throughout the organization. The processes of reviewing performance and planning succession are driven from the top down. You will inevitably be rated and assessed against the same standard of qualities and priorities that your boss was.

Employees with strong world views that differ from the template established by the most senior managers, as a result, are actively or passively culled or weeded out. Succession planning becomes a process of homogenizing the organization rather that promoting the individuals that can contribute most to the company's success by contributing to the diversity of the leadership team.

When I began my career back in the '70s, promotions were often handed out on the basis of seniority and promotion from within was the standard. Those precepts, however, were cast aside long ago in favor of the enticing notion of creating a meritocracy. And, increasingly, the person who wins that meritorious contest is someone from outside the company.

So why are companies continuing to falter at an alarming rate? Why is the average tenure of America's CEOs down to just three years? Why have so many outside saviors flown their companies into the side of the mountain?

Contrary to popular perception, promoting and hiring on the basis of merit will inevitably lead to more homogenization, not less. The traditional practices forced companies to work with what they had. Hiring and promoting on the basis of perceived merit, however, gives the hiring executive or board far more leeway to hire someone that shares their world view.

Like the random walk theory of investing, there is little evidence to show that promoting people on the basis of merit has improved corporate performance to any meaningful degree. It has, however, forced companies to spend more money on hiring bonuses and severance packages.

And it has contributed greatly to disengagement on the job. The reason is simple. Of all the things employees take to heart, fairness is at the top of the list. And if you believe that employees assess their own performance in the same way that the boss does, I have a bridge to sell you.

How often have you heard an executive who has just terminated an employee say, "They weren't surprised"? The implication, of course, is that the decision to terminate was objectively made, and that objectivity is transparent, so everybody knows it.

It is an absurd belief. The terminated employee probably wasn't surprised, because the boss had been subliminally telegraphing the intent for months. I assure you, however, that the employee doesn't share the perception of performance that the company used to rationalize the decision.

Nor will the terminated employee's colleagues. They may support the termination but that support will be a result of how the terminated employee made them feel, not how they performed.

In a future chapter, I will discuss why the corporate meritocracy has failed. And, unfortunately, there is no known cure. I do want to make one more point here, however.

At the NFL combine potential draft prospects are put through a series of tests and evaluations designed to measure strength and athleticism. These include the forty-yard dash, bench press, vertical jump, broad jump, twenty-yard shuttle, three cone drill, and the sixty-yard shuttle, as well as the Cybex test, to test joint movement, and the Wonderlic test, designed to test learning and problem-solving skills. (There is, I should note, significant skepticism that such evaluations truly measure a draftee's future performance potential, but that is not the point here.)

Potential CEOs typically don't have to don their gym shorts and athletic shoes. There are, however, standard protocols that search firms and employers alike employ to "objectively" assess a candidate's potential. Seldom has a C-suite recruiter or sponsoring executive justified a hiring recommendation with, "I just like the way he combs his hair."

The modern notion of business meritocracy is, in the end, merely another step along the continuum of deductive logic. While there is little argument that an individual's business potential can be objectively determined to some degree, it is a potential calibrated by probabilities, not absolutes. We can and have, in my opinion, taken it too far. As in the Tài jí tú symbol, the continuum is wrapping back around on itself. We aren't just failing to realize any incremental benefit; we are contributing to our own failure.

And patting ourselves on the back for our delusions of objectivity as we go.

Nine

Technology

In a quote Mark Twain attributed to British Prime Minister Benjamin Disraeli (1804–1881), Disraeli notes, "There are three kinds of lies: lies, damned lies and statistics." If only he could see us now.

Modern business has never had so much data to process and so many tools to do it with. We can sort data, develop complex analytical models, and convert it all to charts and graphs with the stroke of a few keys.

Information technology has exponentially enhanced our ability to deduce the root causes and influences that drive business success. We no longer have to rely on insight and experience to identify trends or consumer behavior. We can plot them. And we can do so along an almost limitless number of axes simultaneously.

How much of that processing, however, really creates value? Have you watched a baseball game on television lately? Here's a fictitious exchange between two television announcers:

John: Okay, Billy, it's the top of the fourth, and Jimmy Hogan will be the first batter to the plate for the Dragons. He had a single to right in his first at bat and is hitting .323 for the season.

Billy: That's right, John. What I find to be really interesting, though, is that when you consider his hitting in the fourth inning only, his average is .360.

John: You mean, only counting the times he came to bat in the fourth inning?

Billy: Correct. This is the fourth inning after all. And, by the way, if you look at fourth inning at bats during the even months of the season, and this is the fourth inning in an even month, his average jumps to .384. That's impressive.

John: Indeed it is, Billy. I wonder what it was if you only consider fourth inning at bats during the even months when the temperature was above eighty degrees? It is pretty hot out there tonight.

And, of course, Jimmy strikes out because a new pitcher has come into the game that has a slider that Jimmy just can't hit.

What's the point? Does this incremental knowledge really contribute to the viewers' enjoyment of the game? For some, perhaps. For me, however, it's just noise. I much prefer the old days when a single announcer told you the things that you couldn't see on the screen for yourself, but otherwise left you to watch the game.

It also costs the broadcasting network more money, of course. Most televised sporting events now require three or four highly compensated announcers, in part, because one announcer simply can't keep up with both the need for constant chatter and still have the time to digest all of the superfluous statistics being generated in the background by the support team, their heads buried in laptops.

The world of business is not far behind the world of sports. How many fifty-slide PowerPoint presentations did you sit through last week? And how much did you learn or retain?

We live in an era of statistics on steroids. We typically have far more data than we can productively digest, and when we try to distill meaning, we often create an additional opportunity for deception.

In probability theory the law of large numbers holds that the more often you repeat an experiment, the closer the average result will be to the expected value. The same concept holds true in statistical analysis and modeling. The more you parse the data, the more chance there is that the model will provide a false projection. Most companies, for example, will find it easier to forecast aggregate revenue than the sales of each individual stock-keeping unit (SKU).

But the damage done by excessive data analysis and modeling doesn't stop with the dilution of accuracy inherent in more and more detailed modeling. In many ways, the damage is both self-perpetuating and self-enhancing.

One of the reasons is cultural. When computers were first introduced into American business, most companies didn't know what to do with them. The first company I worked for put its first computer—a mainframe computer the size of a car that probably had less computing power than an Apple watch—to work calculating golf handicaps at the company-owned golf course. I kid you not. That's all it was used for because no one could figure out what to do with it.

Eventually, however, the analytical power of computers caught on and companies started to use them in more and more ways. The one phrase you heard again and again, however, in assessing the validity of the computer's work was, "garbage in, garbage out."

You don't hear that phrase much anymore, and I don't think it's because of continued refinement in the quality of the analytical tools available. The reality is that technology is now cool, and there is an assumption that it contributes to business in a positive way.

Consider this: You are interviewing a recent college graduate to fill almost any role in your company other than actor, model, or athlete. And when you ask him about his skills with the Microsoft Office suite, he replies, "Well, I took a course in Excel, but I don't really like to use it because I'm not a big fan of technology. I prefer to do things with pencil and paper. I find the quality of the output to be better because it requires more upfront thought."

Would you hire him? I seriously doubt it. And if you did make the hire, would he be able to compete with his peers that are Excel and PowerPoint wizards for management attention and recognition?

And let's face it; it's easy to while away countless hours expanding your Excel model or prettying up your PowerPoint presentation. It's busy work. And it's a lot less taxing than talking to customers all day, for example.

Perhaps the most pernicious by-product of the modern electronic spreadsheet, however, is the dreaded template. This is the Excel document or online system that corporate and other staff departments send out to all of the operating divisions, departments, or regions, instructing them to populate it with the relevant local data. Common examples involve financial reporting, online performance reviews, succession planning, regulatory compliance, and performance metrics (KPIs)—all of which can then be electronically consolidated and, in many cases, converted to slick-looking dashboards of green, red, and yellow.

In theory, the electronic template is a lot easier to consolidate than the manual spreadsheets of yore, and it allows for a far greater degree of comparative analysis. That's in theory, of course. In reality, the templates never work quite right and the author inevitably locks all of the important cells so that the poor folks who have to populate them can't modify them, even to make them work properly. And, of course, there is seldom consistency in the way each region or division calculates each piece of data to be populated, creating the false impression of an apples-to-apples comparison in the consolidated end product.

The real problem with the electronic template, however, is they are just too easy to create, enabling companies to develop templates and online systems to support global processes that shouldn't exist in the first place. Should the performance appraisal system used in China be the same as the one used in the United States or Europe? Even if you faithfully translate the original document into the local language, you cannot literally translate English into, say, Mandarin. To say nothing about potential cultural considerations.

Many companies use the electronic template to consolidate global operating metrics or KPIs that allow senior executives to see the company's global performance at a glance and to allow local operating regions or divisions to benchmark against each other. But metrics are like language itself. They are manmade protocols designed for efficiency of assessment and communication. They aren't natural in the way that rain and sunshine are. By definition, they are imprecise. Maybe meaningful, maybe not, but the degree to which they are either probably varies over time anyway.

When I was in China, we had several corporate metrics, including several relating to plant safety. We had plants around the world, but the Chinese plant typically posted the best safety metrics. Many outside of China assumed we were fudging the numbers, so we never really got credit for the accomplishment. We weren't cheating, of course, but we did have a young workforce that didn't complain much. The average age of the employees in the US plants was typically decades higher, a fact that wasn't recognized by the safety KPIs.

Which may provide a not so subtle segue into a brief discussion of production process technology, often referred to as automation. Executives, engineers, and investors alike uniformly embrace automation as a way to drive down labor costs, which for many American companies is the number-one internal production cost beyond purchased components, if the process uses them.

Generally speaking, it's fairly easy to create a financial model that supports the investment in automation. Not always, but much of the time. Automation is just another form of process. It can be a very good thing. But it can come with hidden costs that are often overlooked in the initial financial justification.

To the extent that automation results in a loss of operating flexibility, a higher breakeven point, or additional inventory, it may not make sense. Most highly automated processes must be run at or near full capacity to be financially justified. And unless the automation actually contributes to process flexibility, which some does, it doesn't make sense to make more of what you can't sell.

I assumed responsibility for a startup plant once that was highly automated and had very high fixed costs as a percentage of total costs. This was a company that had plants around the world, many of which had been in operation for a long time. A new global manufacturing lead came in and decided that all plant managers, including ours, should focus their efforts on reducing process changeover times, a popular idea at the time. In the case of the startup plant, however, we were still ramping up sales and couldn't sell what we were making. Did it really make sense to put time and effort into reducing changeover times only to have to shut the line down for lack of work?

But I digress. Let's move on to the real scourge of modern technology—the e-mail, the text, and the mobile phone. This discussion is almost superfluous since there is almost no one left in the world of business that doesn't see the problem here. The monster is out of its cage, although few companies are doing anything about it. The amount of time wasted on generating, reading, and reacting to useless, deleterious e-mails and texts is incalculable.

And, of course, it is impossible to unplug from your work, further eroding any hope of achieving any real life-work balance and contributing to the general level of stress in the workplace. France, in late 2016, actually passed a law making it illegal for employees of companies with more than fifty employees to write or receive e-mails outside of preestablished hours.

It is the long-term impact on our ability to communicate, however, that I think poses the greatest threat to business and society at large. In social communication, in particular, it is perfectly acceptable to ignore the rules of grammar, spelling, capitalization, and punctuation. In fact, you can forget about words altogether and just use abbreviations. LOL.

I get it. I really do. But if you think Malcolm Gladwell's ten-thousand-hour rule has any validity, which I think it does in the appropriate context, most of us will be retired before we develop expertise in the more formal written prose generally required in professional environments.

The rules of grammar and punctuation exist for a reason, moreover. There is no global conspiracy of language and writing teachers to annoy school children. The rules have been developed to promote clarity and understanding. They can, of course, compromise efficiency. But that compromise, in the interest of consistency, contributes to standardization, which in turn contributes to understanding. Not always, but standards that are not uniformly applied lose much of their benefit.

I can say without hesitation that one of the most influential professors I had in college was a German economics professor. I don't even remember what course I took from him. But I do remember that he made us write one paper per week with a maximum length of two pages, double-spaced, no exceptions. And the topics were expansive.

It made me think before I wrote, a discipline that served me well when I went to work in the corporate finance department of a multinational consumer-products company at a time before personal computers had even been invented. All correspondence was typed on an electric typewriter, and copies were generally made with carbon paper, the original source of the cc: designation.

If you wanted to maintain any civility with the steno pool, you learned to get it right the first time. Changes were cumbersome to make and compromised the appearance of the finished document.

Along came the word processor and the mouse, of course, and the market for white-out products went the way of the buggy whip. Now you can erase entire documents with the flick of the wrist and a click. It is convenient, to be sure. But it has severely eroded the need to think before you write. Has that, in turn, diluted our ability to focus and to conceptualize our communication before we commit it to paper? I think so. And since so much of our relationships, personal and professional alike, turn on communication, I do wonder what the long-term implications will be.

But this is a topic bigger than this book—perhaps bigger than all books at the moment. Let's defer it to a future discussion.

The point to this book is that technology is the ultimate enabler of our relentless march along the continuum of deductive reasoning. It has momentum and will only slow down when we insist that it does. And that will take an act of supreme induction. Somebody of influence will have to yell, "Enough!"

Ten

Obligation Leadership

N o aspect of business has been more analyzed, debated, and written about than leadership. Without it your business or department may survive, but it won't prosper.

Leadership is not management. The latter is all about telling people what to do. The former is inspiring them to do what you want them to without having to be told.

So, despite all of the attention paid to the topic, why are there so few great business leaders today?

In 2009, author and consultant Simon Sinek gave a delightful TED talk in which he introduced his model for inspirational leadership—the golden circle. His talk went on to become one of the most watched TED talks ever, and if you haven't seen it, I strongly recommend you take a look.

The golden circle that Sinek defines is a series of three concentric circles. The innermost circle represents "why," followed by "how," and "what" as you move out. Most companies and individuals, Sinek contends, focus on the how and the what and never quite get to why. Those who do address the why, such as Steve Jobs and Martin Luther King, two of Sinek's powerful examples, inspire us as a result.

"People don't buy what you do, but why you do it," Sinek notes, adding that Martin Luther King became the face of the civil rights movement because he had a dream, not because he had a plan. It was a dream that many people shared.

The hottest trend in management over the last decade or so has been servant leadership. Almost every CEO talks about the concept. Almost none actually practice it. And the reason is simple: They are focused solely on the how and what of their business and not the why. They're focused on the metrics, the systems, and mining Big Data, not on why they get out of bed in the morning. And certainly not on why their employees and customers should.

Many would say that management exists to serve the shareholders. I don't buy it. That's like saying the gamblers own the casino. Profits are a result, not a reason for being. Profits are the equivalent of breathing. We must do it, but breathing itself won't sustain the soul.

When it comes to organizational leadership, the most powerful why is obligation in all its many forms. An obligation is a responsibility. If a leader is obligated to the employees in his or her care, the leader is assuming responsibility for both their performance and for their job fulfillment.

I can already hear the cries of "foul." You can't be held accountable for the fulfillment of the employees you manage, right? And, to an extent, that's true. People have to take ownership of their own happiness.

But that misses the real point. If your employees do find fulfillment in their work, they are going to perform at a higher level. One—the quality of life—leads to the other—the quality of work. And isn't that what you want?

The thing that links them is trust. Trust is the secret sauce that empowers us to perform at our best; to take risks; and to eliminate the waste of worry, doubt, and posturing.

But here's where obligation transcends trust: Obligation is a two-way street. It's dynamic. Obligation begets obligation. If I believe in the sincerity of your obligation to me, I am naturally compelled to return that obligation. I am obliged. And that, in the end, is the very definition of true teamwork.

Back to Sigmund Freud and his insightful observation that all of life is personal. I think Sinek would agree. We do things for ourselves. Not because someone told us to or someone is paying us to. Those are just jobs. We do things because we want to, because we believe that following this leader will provide personal satisfaction and fulfillment. And we'll never achieve that unless the leaders give us a reason to trust them.

Trust and sincerity are kissin' cousins. People will never trust you unless they first believe you are sincere. To lead by obligation, you must be truly willing to put the self-interests of those you seek to lead ahead of your own. Do you pass that test? Does your boss?

That's worth repeating: *You must be willing to put the self-interests of those you seek to lead ahead of your own.* Too much? Unrealistic? Just plain insane?

You might be tempted to throw my own logic right back at me and point out that the leadership relationship does not exist in isolation. As a leader you also have an obligation to yourself and your family. And that is true. But why do these obligations have to be mutually exclusive?

If you are a parent, do you put obligation to your children above your obligation to self? Most parents do. It's how we're wired. But maybe it's not how we're wired in the way we think. Is parental obligation selfless or selfish?

Psychologists will tell you that one of the first things a parent says to a newborn child is, "I am not going to do _____ to you, like my parents did to me." But the child won't know if you made good on the commitment or not. The only one who will knowingly benefit is you. You have the chance to correct a perceived injustice that you suffered. What could be more personal than that?

Educators will tell you that one of the best ways to insure a child gets a good education is parental involvement in the process. And why do parents get involved? Because that's what parents are supposed to do? And why are they supposed to? Is it because parents want to raise children that they can be proud of and that will reflect positively on them? That's pretty selfish, don't you think?

Or have we made this into a false dilemma fallacy? Is it really either/or? Or can I be a good parent and get something out of it at the same time?

Not convinced? Let's look at it from the child's perspective. Your mother or father got fired from her or his very good job because she or he went to bat against a company decision that she or he believed was unjust to its employees. Are you angry or proud? Do you feel that parent reneged on an obligation to you as a parent, or did that parent teach you by their example a lesson that you will remember throughout your life?

I don't need to ask how the parent felt. Yes, a job was lost, and the future is uncertain. I can guarantee, however, that the pride of having done the right thing will far outweigh any sense of defeat or failure.

You can never go wrong doing the right thing. That is a universal and timeless truth. And doing the right thing is just the action tense of obligation.

So, yes, I am indeed serious when I say that to be a true leader you must put the interests of those you lead above your own. You must be willing to sacrifice.

Do you remember Maslow's hierarchy of needs? The third level in the hierarchy is the need for connection. And you must achieve that before you can achieve esteem and self-actualization, the fourth and fifth levels.

But are you connected if you're just caught on the bumper of the car and dragged down the street? Or does the connection have to be a mutual connection before it can lead to esteem and self-actualization? And how do you achieve mutual connection without mutual obligation and trust?

Talk, of course, is cheap. Obligation and trust are meaningless if they aren't sincere—and perceived as such. Insincere obligation is not returned and, therefore, fails to provide connection. And that, of course, means that esteem and self-actualization are out of the question.

Most business executives today, of course, have been extensively coached in the need for sincerity. And many work hard to put on a convincing face. Most, however, ultimately fail.

In part this is due to the fact that the selflessness of obligation doesn't come easy to many of us. We believe it's counterintuitive because we haven't framed the issue in the right context. Once again, we've fallen victim to the false dilemma, the either/or argument so common in the modern communication we're exposed to every day.

It's tough to get away with false sincerity over time. I strongly advise against trying. People have an intuitive sense when it comes to sincerity. Just like a dog can smell fear, so, too, can your employees tell when you are sincere and when you aren't. And just like the animals, people will ultimately attack when they smell your insincerity. You may fend them off initially, but you won't once they become a pack.

The important thing to remember is that people don't judge sincerity by what you say. They judge what you do. Your behavior is the ultimate tell, as a poker player might say. You can hide behind your words, but your actions uncloak your true convictions. If a picture is worth a thousand words, your behavior is worth ten thousand pictures.

Employment in the United States is largely governed by the doctrine of employment at will. It is a doctrine enforced by common law that presumes that employment is voluntary for the employer and the employee. If not, employees would be akin to indentured servants. And given America's historical obsession with the ideal of free markets, it is no surprise that the courts have historically enforced a quid pro quo. If employees can leave voluntarily, the employer must have the same right to dismiss them.

There are exceptions, of course, that are generally a function of other legal contracts that bind both parties. And recent legislation has given some protection to certain classes of employees that might otherwise be targets of discrimination. On balance, however, the employer still holds the upper hand. If an employer wants you to leave, it will find a way to make it happen.

Nonetheless, an informal social contract generally existed between employee and employer up until the 1980s. It essentially held that if an employee worked hard, did their best, and didn't violate the law, the employer would only terminate or lay them off under the most extreme circumstances.

That informal understanding, however, was unilaterally cast aside by most employers with the advent of shareholder activism and the surge in equity compensation in the late twentieth century. Based on subsequent behavior, few employees today are naïve enough to believe that the employer will hesitate to throw them all under the bus at the first sign of financial trouble or to enhance a depressed stock price.

Not surprisingly, trust is a rare commodity in most business organizations today. And corporate performance has suffered as a result.

I took over my first operating division at the age of thirty-two. While I felt more than qualified for the position at the time, I look back three decades later and wonder what the senior leadership team was thinking. I made a lot of mistakes.

But I never considered that I was putting my job in jeopardy. The leadership of that company led by sincere obligation, and, as a result, I trusted them. I was empowered to take risks. Big risks. And despite my many failures, some of those big risks paid off. And I would eventually become president of the entire company.

Peter Drucker is often credited with saying, "Culture eats strategy for lunch every day." It's true. And the difference between a constructive culture and a destructive culture is trust—the inevitable by-product of leadership obligation.

Eleven

The Law of Unintended Consequence

The law of unintended consequence (LOUC) holds that all change results in consequences that were unforeseen at the time a decision was made. "Be careful what you wish for" and the "self-fulfilling prophecy" are variations on the same theme.

There are endless examples. When alcohol was made illegal during Prohibition, it gave rise to a powerful and ruthless class of violent bootleggers. And otherwise law-abiding citizens chose to become criminals as their respect for the rule of law dwindled, undoubtedly undermining their respect for all laws and all law enforcement. In the end Americans decided that these unintended costs outweighed the benefits, and Prohibition was abolished. Good intent, bad outcome.

In a similar vein, when the government passes regulations to license certain professions in the name of consumer and worker protection, they are concurrently creating a de facto oligopoly that ultimately drives up prices. It is entirely plausible, as a result, that consumers will forego the cost of a licensed practitioner and either skip the repair or improvement or do it on their own.

The Food and Drug Administration, in its attempt to insure the safety of drugs entering the market, has, in turn, been criticized for slowing down the introduction of new drugs and increasing their market price. In the extreme people suffering from a certain disease may have died waiting for FDA approval. And, of course, pharmaceutical companies are financially discouraged from developing life-saving drugs for diseases that are not widespread due to the cost of getting FDA approval.

Unintended consequences can be equally catastrophic in the world of business. Managers and executives often introduce new policies and plans that are well intended in their design but ultimately lead to disaster. Again, the examples are endless.

When investors insisted that the executives of public corporations be given compensation packages that are more aligned with the interests of shareholders, they got exactly what they asked for. What they also created, however, was the most polarized corporate compensation structure in history. While CEOs can now make tens of millions of dollars per year, largely through stock options and grants, the wages of the average worker have risen only modestly.

And while the US stock market is currently soaring to record levels, there is little evidence that this is the result of enriching corporate executives in the name of shareholder alignment. The practice has, however, certainly contributed to the stark emotional and political divisions that currently run through American society.

In another all too familiar example of unintended consequence, the Internet has put the world at our fingertips. But it has also put everyone at the fingertips of criminals and terrorists, an unforeseen consequence that most Internet pioneers now admit they never anticipated.

Rewarding professional athletes with market-driven compensation packages has made the process more fair to the athletes, but it has also driven up the cost of attending most professional sporting events, putting many beyond the reach of the average consumer and furthering the American economic divide.

During the Vietnam War, college students received automatic deferrals from the draft in the name of social need. Not surprisingly, a subsequent report from the US Census Bureau found that the college enrollment rate for eighteen- to twenty-four-year-old men rose from

24 percent in 1960 to 36 percent in 1969, dropping dramatically in the mid-1970s. (The last draftee was inducted in 1973.) And because college attendance correlates with family income and wealth, a disproportionate number of soldiers fighting in the jungles of Vietnam came from economically disadvantaged families. They ultimately discontinued the college deferment once the unintended consequence became obvious to all.

The Founding Fathers of the United States believed strongly in democratic ideals but were wary of giving pure democratic majorities too much power and thus allowing absolute pluralities to exploit numerical minorities. As a result, two political institutions were created—the Electoral College and the US Senate. In the case of the US Senate, each state was granted the same representation of two senators regardless of the population of the state.

The Electoral College, of course, creates the potential, as we saw in 2016, for a presidential candidate to receive a plurality of the popular vote but lose the election. It is a relatively common occurrence, in fact, dating back to 1824, when John Quincy Adams defeated Andrew Jackson despite having lost the popular vote. (The House of Representatives ultimately decided that election as neither candidate gained a majority in the Electoral College.)

Much of the work of the US Senate is accomplished in its twenty committees. Committee chairs, as a result, wield enormous power. And, at the moment, the chairmen of the five most powerful Senate committees (Appropriations, Finance, Armed Services, Judiciary, and Foreign Relations) hail from states (Mississippi, Utah, Arizona, Iowa, and Tennessee, respectively) that collectively account for only 7 percent of the total US population.

Why? Committee leadership is assigned by seniority and the more populous states are more aggressively contested by both political parties, typically providing the elected leaders of the less populated states more tenure. And, as an unintended consequence of that, the less populous states tend to receive a disproportionate share of federal government expenditures compared to the amount of money contributed by their taxpayers. Of the five states referenced above, only the citizens of Utah pay more in federal taxes that they receive in federal benefits.

In the world of business, the impact of the unintended consequence is even more pronounced, in large part because the process of managing a business today is typically built on a foundation of deductive logic. When every decision is statistically analyzed and financially modeled, there is an inherent tendency to weigh fewer variables more heavily than others due to the simple fact that not all variables can be easily identified or quantified. Statistically, this creates a greater cost penalty from unintended consequences that are underweighted in the analysis.

Said differently, in a world where deductive reason is given disproportionate consideration, the negative impact of bad decisions will be disproportionately greater. Which is one of the root causes of declining CEO tenure in the United States. The average CEO in the United States holds his or her job for only three years, on average, due, in part, to the increasing emphasis on deductive thinking by CEOs and their boards.

I began my career in a period of relatively high inflation in the United States. (My first mortgage carried an interest rate of 17 percent.) People were sensitive to the issue and my first employer, an old company with a very paternalistic culture, deliberately gave the same absolute wage increase (e.g., thirty-five cents per hour) to all hourly employees regardless of the job they performed. The rationale was noble; the price of bread had gone up by the same amount for everyone.

Over time, however, there was obvious compression in the wage structure. The premium paid to the most highly skilled employees was significantly less than it had once been. And the skilled employees weren't happy, a problem for which there was no attractive solution.

The mortgage crisis of 2008 did not take the world by surprise. It took many by surprise, but some investors correctly understood the unintended consequences and made fortunes off their insight. Why didn't we listen? What did they know that the regulators and the big banks didn't?

The simple answer is that nobody wanted to know. Too many people were simply making too much money, and there were no victims. Until the collapse there was no aggrieved party. The room was full of winners.

The root cause of the eventual collapse, I believe, was the illusion created by the conceptual singularity of deductive logic. The false allure of deductive logic is the misguided perception that logic can exist in a single dimension, that deductive conclusions can be isolated and stand on their own. It's a myth.

For every yin there is a yang. For every pro there is a con. It's as fundamental as that. No decision or behavior has a singular consequence. Outcome is never one-dimensional. There are multiple ramifications of every action taken by every business every hour of the day. The only question is whether they are anticipated or arrive like a surprise guest.

Every part of the mortgage play that resulted in the global financial meltdown of 2008 was supported by sophisticated financial models that made the whole process appear very objective and financially justified. The banks had models that supported the market for the collateralized mortgage obligations (CMOs) they were selling to gleeful investors. The ratings agencies had models that supported their claims that the CMOs were safe. And the insurers had models that supported their contention that default rates would be acceptable. And they were all wrong.

And the saddest truth of all is that all it would have taken for all of the huge corporations involved to understand the risk of the whole scheme was a little inductive logic along the lines of, "This is simply too good to be true." And it was.

It wasn't the only time business executives have been lured into inductively ridiculous decisions by the siren's song of deductive logic. In the early 1990s, Hoover, the venerable provider of home-cleaning products, including vacuums, ran a promotion in the United Kingdom that ultimately cost the company tens of millions of dollars and the marketing executives responsible for the idea their jobs.

The idea wasn't new; the devil was in the details. Consumers who bought a vacuum for ninety-nine pounds received two free airline tickets for travel to Europe or the United States as a gift. Not surprisingly, vacuum sales took off, if you'll excuse the pun. But people weren't buying the vacuums; they were indirectly buying the airline tickets. Consumers stuck the vacuums in the closet or gave them to a friend and flew to Disney World with their family.

Simple. The marketers who launched the promotion put their faith in their financial model. They didn't consider that their financial assumptions were absurd. In short, they assumed the average claim rate experienced in a large sampling of gift-with-purchase promotions without ever considering the relative value of the product and the gift.

The heightened sense of accountability that exists in corporate America today exacerbates the potentially devastating impact of the LOUC. Employees are intuitively aware of the LOUC and its potential consequences. At a certain level that is exactly how children learn. We can't learn what we already know. It is the LOUC that exposes us to the new truth that we didn't expect.

In a very sense, the LOUC is a close relative of fear. Everyone understands that risk is a fundamental building block of life. We smell it, we feel it, and we hear it. Nobody needs to be reminded that life is fragile and success is tenuous.

That is why it is counterproductive for corporate leaders to spend too much time and effort harping on the need for accountability and performance. People get it. The need for accountability and performance are not confined to the workplace.

If a company wants to move forward in these tumultuous times, it must strike a balance in its narrative around accountability. You cannot scare people into behaving the way you want. You cannot convince them through talk alone. You cannot guide their behavior through even the clearest explanation of your expectations.

Human emotion is inductive in nature. You can't deductively find love. You may deductively enhance the chances of achieving it, but the final leap is decidedly inductive.

If you want to engage and motivate your employees, you can't rely solely on the tools of deduction any more than you can rely solely on the analytics of deduction to make smart business decisions. Context is often inductive. And context is where both the quality of decisions and the quality of life find expression.

Twelve

Communication

Linguists break communication styles the world over into two groups. Some cultures are transmitter oriented, wherein the speaker has the responsibility for the effectiveness of the communication. Some are receiver-oriented, where the responsibility falls with the listener.

Conceptually, it makes sense that those cultures built on a foundation of deductive logic (e.g., Western), moving from left to right, are transmitter oriented. Cultures built on a foundation of inductive logic (e.g., Chinese) are generally more receiver oriented.

That's why a Westerner who walks into a Chinese supermarket on a Sunday afternoon has an immediate impulse to flee. The market is filled with an army of hawkers all shouting through tinny portable speakers at the same time. It is noise pollution in the extreme. But the Chinese don't appear to notice. And that is because the hawkers are simply not there until the Chinese shoppers choose to listen. They literally don't hear them.

This is also the reason that Americans traveling abroad often resort to speaking loudly if they are struggling to get their point across to someone who does not share their language. And, no, in my experience volume has no impact on fluency.

The net result is that Americans are typically not very astute listeners. As a former colleague of mine used to ask, "Are you listening to respond or listening to understand?" Most of us are doing the former most of the time. We are practicing precognitive response. We are picking out only the words that we believe are essential to forming a response. In some cases, we are not listening at all because we have already framed some form of response based on our previous assessment of the transmitter.

Or as transmitters we have a list of talking points we want to make regardless of the questions asked. Politicians do this all the time. Corporate executives do as well. The actual questions asked by an audience of reporters, employees, or investors are mere cues for the speaker to regurgitate the next point on the list.

Albert Mehrabian, a UCLA researcher, performed several studies in the late 1960s that ultimately gave rise to what is commonly referred to as the 7-38-55 rule. It holds that words themselves account for only 7 percent of the effectiveness of communication while tone and body language account for 38 percent and 55 percent, respectively.

If I am on an airplane anywhere in the world, when the flight attendant rolls the beverage cart down the aisle, hands me a napkin and a bag of snacks, and asks me a question, I am fluent in every language under the sun. The language he or she is speaking is irrelevant. The question is always the same: "What would you like to drink?" The context says it all.

When I was working in China and meeting with the head of the Labor Bureau, who spoke no English, I could nonetheless assume that the official was not discussing taxes, fire prevention, or the environment. The topic surely involved issues of labor.

I could further interpret whether the official was happy or unhappy about whatever labor issue based on body language. Anger is easy to spot. But, with practice, you can also interpret more subtle expressions of the gravity of the communication through the same assessment of body language.

Having thus narrowed the potential topics down to just a few, I didn't have to understand many of the actual words used to correctly interpret meaning and intent. Even though my fluency in Mandarin was limited, I could communicate.

Which is why I often encourage students who are learning a foreign language to put as much effort into becoming a good listener as they put into speaking the new language. The universe of words you must consider in your communication is reduced considerably if you listen effectively.

Context is also why Americans tend to listen more receptively to someone of recognized authority or fame than, say, the man begging for spare change on the sidewalk. When a celebrity speaks, people will attribute far greater wisdom and insight to the comments than they probably deserve. Some celebrities are brilliant. But some say the most inane things. In both cases, however, they are likely to have their audience hanging on every word, the precognitive expectation being that important people only say important things. It is, of course, a crock.

Communication bias, of course, is a huge problem for the business executive. The biggest barrier to effectiveness for most corporate executives is isolation. They do not have direct involvement in most of the day to day activities of the organization, the information they do receive tends to come from just a few sources, and that information is inevitably filtered in a way to promote the best interests of the transmitter.

But this is not a risk limited to the C-suite. It is a pandemic throughout the entire organization. Which is why lower level employees often feel very much in the dark or believe that those above them are truly clueless.

The biggest reason that business communication is so ineffective today, however, is that the way we communicate in a business setting mirrors the way we approach our business. In short, it is decidedly deductive.

Just as all communication can be classified as transmitter oriented or receiver oriented, all communication can also be classified as deductive or inductive. But there is a counterintuitive twist.

The deductive transmitter is worried about how the communication will be interpreted. They assume that their communication will be deductively parsed and want to ensure that doesn't create a potential legal or social liability. Which is why deductive transmitters use a lot of weasel words. Words are important.

Inductive transmitters, on the other hand, care less about exactly what they say. They are more cognizant of the context of the communication than the words themselves. The language they use, as a result, can be more colorful and descriptive. (And potentially less accurate if taken out of context.) The words matter less.

Which is why the talking heads on television in America spend so much time fretting over what some politician did or did not actually say. Such communication, to their way of thinking, is filled with hidden meaning. Words matter.

Early in my time in China, my family returned to Beijing from a beach holiday in Thailand. The Chinese woman who worked in our home was there when we arrived. And she was obviously happy to see us. She turned to my American wife, however, and said with a giggle, "Oh, you are a little fat." She even reached out and touched my wife's stomach to insure she understood.

The message intended, of course, was not the message received. The Chinese woman was suggesting that my wife must have enjoyed very good food while away, a happy and complimentary sentiment given the importance the Chinese put on food and dining. My wife, of course, took it as a slight and immediately backed away from the touch.

Maya Angelou (1928–2014), the noted American poet, actress, and American Civil Rights leader, remarked as follows:

I've learned that people will forget what you said, people will forget what you did, but people will never forget how you made them feel.

In 2010, *Forbes* asked ten CMOs and advertising experts to identify the best-ever advertising taglines. Here are their top five:

1. The Ultimate Driving Machine (BMW)
2. Just Do It (Nike)
3. Don't Leave Home Without It (American Express)
4. We Try Harder (Avis)
5. Got milk? (California Milk Processor Board)

(*Forbes*, Ken Bruno, Contributor, May 29, 2010)

And what do these five taglines all have in common? They all use the language of induction. None of them attempt to provide detailed deductive reasons to explain why they are better. Each appeals to a sentiment. Without that appeal, in fact, they are all just empty constructs of meaningless words.

But this is the language of advertising agencies, not the language employed by most business executives. Read any quote from any CEO in the United States included in any earnings release of any US public corporation that has failed to meet expectations, and you will quickly conclude that it could have been uttered by Uber Dork, the infamous teacher in *Ferris Bueller's Day Off* (1986). It is devoid of emotion. And that's the intent.

The corporate legal community hasn't helped. The language of induction is open to interpretation. In theory, at least, the language of deduction is not. And lawyers loathe uncertainty. Which is why no respectable lawyer would ever ask a witness in a court trial a question that the lawyer didn't already know the answer to.

Deduction and induction are the yin and yang of reason. Deductively, they complement each other. Inductively, theirs is an embrace of love or hate.

If you have trouble sleeping tonight, go to sec.gov, the official website of the Securities and Exchange Commission, and read any randomly selected 10-K or 10-Q. (Forms that companies must file with the SEC at the end of the year and quarter, respectively.) If it doesn't put you to sleep, you might be tempted to jump out the window.

They are uniformly boring. Only the numbers have real meaning, and that's only because there are regulatory limits on how much latitude a company has with its numbers. The text is largely uninformative, both because it is bland and because you can't absorb truth if you can't concentrate while in the grip of ennui.

The language of deduction has also given us political correctness. It is based on the idea that all words have meaning, and those meanings are very precise. Essentially, political correctness discounts context. And understanding context, of course, is the most important ingredient of effective communication.

In this respect, political correctness is actually self-defeating. Politically correct people don't say what they mean so much as they say what can be deductively defended. They parse their words. This word is correct; this word is not.

It is no surprise, therefore, that as American business and society has marched along the continuum of deduction its communication has become both less informative and more politically correct. Both results flow from the same cause—the language of deduction.

Which is a good part of the reason why Americans are so politically divided and so resentful and disillusioned. The language of deduction is the language of isolation. And as Maslow pointed out, and most religions reinforce, we are built for connection, not isolation. Few animals in the world spend their life in isolated solitude.

And, as is common to transmitter-oriented cultures, the less we sense that our message is getting through, the louder we get. Rallies and protests are now commonplace. Constituents aren't listening to their elected officials. They're yelling at them, virtually prohibiting any sincere attempt on the part of the official to actually communicate.

Why are hate groups on the rise again? Hate is inductive. It thrives on the language of induction. And could it be that by squeezing the language of induction out of our public discourse we are enflaming the induction that resides on the margins, roiling the prejudice of racism and misogyny.

Said differently, is not the march toward absolute deduction compelling us to listen to respond rather than listen to learn? In terms of effectiveness, our listening skills are deteriorating, and it may likely be that the more education we receive the more true that is.

One of the questions I am frequently asked about my experience in China is how I could manage people whose language I did not speak. And the answer is that the situation forced me to become a much better listener. Pavlovian responses simply aren't possible under the circumstances. You are forced to listen to learn first. You have no choice.

If you've ever watched a video of the US president meeting with a foreign counterpart, you have surely noticed the person sitting behind each leader. These are the translators. They are both translating the dialogue and taking notes of their impression of comments that don't lend themselves to literal translation.

I used translators often during my time in China. At first it was very cumbersome. The conversation, by definition, is much slower than it is when both speak the same language. And, at first, I found that this impeded pace was the source of some anxiety on my part. I just wanted to get on with it.

Over time, however, I came to truly appreciate the value of the translated conversation, even once I acquired enough proficiency in the language to understand much of what was said. And that's because I ultimately realized that the translated conversation made me a better listener. I had time to digest what the speaker had said and to formulate my thoughts. To the point, actually, that I would defer to the translator even when it wasn't necessary simply to buy myself time to think.

The crux of all this discussion around communication is that if you want to have a more successful career or a more fulfilling life, you merely need to put as much effort into listening as you put into transmitting. And on both ends of that continuum is the language of induction. If you communicate inductively, you will be more effective in getting your point across. If you listen inductively, you will truly learn.

For every meeting you hold on talent management or strategic planning, therefore, make sure you spend an equal amount of time teaching the organization the skills of effective listening. One efficacious trick, as I learned quite by accident, is to expose yourself to people who don't speak your language fluently. If offered a chance to relocate overseas, jump at it. If your colleague speaks English as a second language, spend time with him or her.

It is, of course, an uphill battle given the surge in the use of e-mail, texting, and the most feckless form of communication of all, the tweet. They are two-dimensional, impersonal, and totally lacking of context. Just moving the needle back toward the face-to-face conversation will greatly impact the effectiveness of our communication.

The greatest impact on the effectiveness of our communication, however, will come from our willingness to reembrace the language of induction and seeking a greater balance between our perceptions of what is politically correct and what is not, between our transmitter-oriented communication and our receiver-oriented communication, between our desire to respond and our desire to learn, between the yin and yang of our effort to communicate.

Thirteen

Meritocracy

The American workplace is billed as a meritocracy. It's not. But that is neither a complaint nor a criticism any more than is the observation that you can't choose the family, or the country, or even the era, that you are born into.

Early in my adult life I developed an interest for racing sailboats. And if you want to race a sailboat, you are advised to pick the class of boat that has the most robust following in your area. You can't hone your skills as a race captain if there is no one to race against.

For me that was the Comet class, a two-person dinghy with a retractable centerboard that was originally developed as a training boat for the larger Star class. The Star is a two-person sloop-rigged keelboat raced in the Summer Olympics from 1932 to 2012. It was dropped, however, for the 2016 Summer Olympics in Rio.

At one Comet regatta I attended, I walked among the competing boats as their owners prepared their boats on land before putting them in the water for the races ahead. And when I came upon the boat belonging to one of the best sailors in the class, I noticed that he had written a message to himself on his boom, right in front of where his face would be for much of the race.

It said, "The harder I work the luckier I get." The message struck home.

In sailing, the best sailors inevitably win over any given stretch of time. Any sailor, however, can win any single race. The wind can be very fluky on the small inland lakes where most Comet class regattas are held. And if you are fortunate enough to be at the right place at the right time, such shifts can propel you ahead of the fleet. Or knock you to the back, depending on your fortunes for the day.

I admit that I was not a particularly skillful racer. I rationalized, therefore, that I should sail to the opposite side of the course from that chosen by the most skilled sailors, who could use their skills to make their boats go faster than I could. They were probably correct in their selection, owing to their greater talent in making such decisions, but I wasn't going to win if they were anyway. I might as well bet the farm, as they say, on the off chance that they were wrong.

And a few times I was right—or lucky, depending on your perspective. I went to the far side of the course and sailed to victory, not because I was sailing faster than anyone else but because I had to travel less distance to reach the finish line, the benefactor of a significant but apparently unexpected shift in wind direction.

Pundits often employ a similar strategy in making projections about things that no one can ever really know for sure. Whether it is the long-term direction of the economy, the price of gold, or future geopolitical unrest, it's not a bad strategy until you gain some actual fame and following. Until then, if you're wrong few people will notice. If you are right, however, you can boast the fact on the jacket of your new book, and people may well buy it.

This is not, however, a strategy I recommend for your business career. Few careers are built on a single event, and your boss will have a sense of history that a book buyer may not have perusing potential books to buy at the local bookstore.

We've all heard the naysayers at every company greet a new idea with the claim, "We tried that before and it didn't work." Fair enough. That's good to know.

I once worked with an incessantly optimistic marketing executive who would frequently make that same negative observation when a new idea was put on the table. He always followed it, however, with the caveat, "But good marketing ideas are sometimes good ideas at the wrong time."

The same goes for great employees. Everyone, I believe, has the potential to be both great and inefficacious—the hero and the chump. No one is immune. And most of us, myself included, are both at different points in our career—or even the past week.

Which is why I have such a strong aversion to the popular notion that organizations should constantly cull the worst performers in their ranks. The idea assumes—always a mistake—that personal performance is both measurable and identifiable. And it assumes, moreover, that you have objectively measured that performance in the proper context of place and time.

I have served on the board of directors of four different public companies and held the position of president, CEO, or general manager of another three. And each of those experiences reinforced in me the conviction that when it comes to measuring individual performance in any organization, objectivity is the worst kind of myth.

It is also a myth that people are promoted or terminated based on performance. In fact, this may be the biggest myth of all. That's not to say people who are promoted aren't worthy of the promotion or that people who are identified to have performance issues don't have areas in which they need to improve. It's only to say that there's always more to the story.

Some part of that story, of course, is the self-interest of the individual assessing the performance. They are biased. In some cases, they are very biased. The only real question is in which direction that bias points them. That doesn't make us all bad managers; it makes us human.

In any business organization of more than a handful of people, it's impossible to sort out who is contributing exactly what to either the success or the failure of the company. As the Taoists might say, it is just too complicated for our feeble minds to comprehend. Business, like life, is just too intricate.

There are many companies that have flown into the side of the proverbial mountain over the course of time. And many of those were losing altitude for a very long time indeed. Yet board after board after board did nothing to replace management that was underperforming by any objective measure. Why?

And why do boards allow historically successful CEOs to make calamitous mistakes about acquisitions or bold new strategies when nearly every one of its members have doubts about the wisdom of the decision? I assure you it happens daily.

When all is said and done, the context within which all performance evaluations are conducted is trust. And when it's not, you don't want to work there anyway.

Think about it. Trust is a prerequisite to hope, confidence, and faith. It is the foundation of all success in virtually every field of endeavor.

Trust lives on the border between yin and yang. John Donne (1572–1631) coined the phrase, "No man is an island..." Nothing, as the Buddhists believe, exists in isolation. And it is that border with the people and the universe around us that is defined by trust.

In any relationship, moreover, whether it is between friends or colleagues, it is trust that bridges the gap between the deductive and the inductive. It is trust, or the lack thereof, that bridges observation and assessment in matters of human performance.

This truth plays out in many dimensions. Your boss will not evaluate your performance favorably if he does not trust you. You cannot effectively collaborate with a colleague if trust is not established first. You, most importantly, can never realize your full potential if you are not trustworthy.

But trust is a fickle thing. It can evaporate in the blink of an eye. And it is never an illusion. Acting trustworthy is not at all the same as being trustworthy. Trust sometimes takes sacrifice. A leader must occasionally make an unpopular decision in the interest of trust. But trust demands allegiance; it does not play second fiddle.

In theory, there is nothing wrong with assessing performance in the workplace. It can be effective and productive. It can help employees to grow, and it is a prerequisite to effective succession planning and organizational development.

You must first, however, establish an environmental context of trust. Without it, all will be lost. You cannot manage your talent if you don't have their trust first. Your efforts will be futile. Or, more likely, they will backfire. Your most talented people will destroy you.

Trust, in the end, is an inductive emotion that generally begins with a deductive assessment. It is where we land when we take that leap of faith that theologians talk about being necessary to becoming a true believer. It is the connection between what we observe in a person and how we feel about them. It is the cornerstone of both extraordinary performance and unshakeable dedication.

Why are some team athletes able to perform beyond their normal abilities in an important game? Is it for the glory? The prize? No. They do it for the team.

Why are soldiers willing to die in battle? Do they do it for their country, their flag, or the values they hold dear? No. They do it for their buddies.

As I discussed in chapter 5, connection is the secret sauce of personal fulfillment. And personal fulfillment is the singular path to realizing your full potential. Maslow called it self-actualization—the pinnacle of the hierarchy of human needs.

But if effective talent management requires a foundation of trust, the process itself can both reinforce and weaken that foundation. The key is whether you view the process as deductive or inductive. To be effective, it must be a little of both.

Assessments of attitude, teamwork, collaboration, and the willingness to embrace change are all essentially inductive. You may be able to produce real life examples to support your assessment, but that assessment is, at its core, subjective. Most people are all of these things and none of them at different times. (Human performance and attitude oscillate to the sine wave like everything else.) It all comes down to which picture you want to pick out of the collage.

That doesn't make those judgments bad. I happen to think they are important. The person you are assessing will know they are judgments. But it's always helpful to know the judgments that your boss has made, subjective or not.

When you try to force the inductive into the hard confines of the deductive, however, you inevitably undermine trust, and in doing so you cripple the process. Even the talent suffers.

One example of this is the forced bell curve, as discussed previously. (I can't overemphasize its lunacy.) In theory, it may make sense. In reality, it destroys trust. The bell curve is a manifestation of probability theory. A fundamental law of probability theory, however, is the law of large numbers, discussed in chapter 9, which holds that the larger the data pool, the closer the average result will get to the expected value.

A department of ten is hardly a large data pool. A company of two hundred is still a puddle. One thousand is a small pond. And ten thousand is big enough to start behaving like an ocean, but even it is not big enough to actually be an ocean.

The biggest mistake most companies make, however, is coupling the performance review with the annual salary adjustment, particularly if that adjustment is material or there are material differences in the adjustments given. Forget about managing talent if you do. You have pushed performance underground and severely compromised the trust that binds an effective organization.

That's not to suggest that everyone should always get the same increase. It is to say, however, that managing and developing your talent is not the same thing as rewarding and compensating your talent. They are different processes.

My father grew up in the mountains of northern New Hampshire, so it's no surprise that he taught his children to ski at a young age. And it's also no surprise that as an adolescent I was generally embarrassed when I fell down on the slope. To which my father would inevitably respond, "If you aren't falling, you aren't getting better," which is why he always encouraged me to ski with friends who were more advanced than I was.

When I entered an actual race, however, he didn't wish me to fall down on the course. He wanted me to push my limits, for sure, but he wanted me to know the fulfillment of success and that would only happen if I finished the race.

It's not a perfect analogy, for sure. But I think it does speak to the difference between managing and developing talent and giving out recognition and reward—managing your compensation structure.

The point is not to try and make talent management an exclusively deductive process. Don't be afraid of either the language or the emotion of induction. It is where we live. And it is where we excel and we fail. It is the keystone of both dedication and excellence.

And who will be your best talent managers? That's simple: your most optimistic managers. Optimism is a dimension of trust. Optimistic people both trust and instill trust in others. An article posted on the Stanford Encyclopedia of Trust website notes, "Failing to be optimistic about people's competence also makes trust impossible."

It's another facet of precognitive conclusion, I suppose. The people you manage will perform as you expect them to. Give them the benefit of the doubt, and they will grow to trust you. Build that trust, and you will unleash their true potential. And both of you will be rewarded.

Fourteen

Instinct

As the modern business community has come increasingly to believe that management is more science than art, data and the analytical tools used to interpret it have increased greatly in perceived importance. This, of course, has been reinforced by the advancement of technology that has put more and more data at our fingertips while providing more and more quick and easy ways to massage it.

Not surprisingly, given our predilection to digital choices, and the general but invalid belief that science is absolute, instinct has fallen out of fashion. It is commonly considered to be arbitrary, uninformed, unprofessional, and, of course, ineffective.

I would argue, however, that there is a place—a necessary place—for instinct and intuition. And here's why.

The business executive has two overriding enemies—misinterpretation and false rationalization. Both can and often do lead to bad decisions about strategy, investment, and staffing.

There are two facets to the world of communication that business leaders rely upon to make informed decisions. One is the alphabetical—written and verbal. The other is numeric—statistical and analytical.

The problem with language, as I have noted throughout, is that it is an invented mechanism for assisting in effective and timely communication. It is no more or less than a body of symbols designed to facilitate understanding.

As a result, we all know that language is often ineffective. Reality is simply too complex to lend itself to symbolic representation. That's why we need poems, novels, and the lyrics of song.

In China that truth is obvious. The same set of Chinese characters can mean many things, so a Chinese conversation may seem inexplicably long for the simple question or statement first offered. That is because both parties to the communication must typically ask follow up questions to understand context, and thus discover the true intent of the communication.

Numbers, despite their prominence in the world of science, and the aura of objectivity that bestows upon them, are equally symbolic. Econometricians have developed elaborate and complex computer models to simulate real-life commerce in quantitative ways. And some provide the right answers some of the time. No one, however, has ever translated the true complexity of commercial reality into zeroes and ones. No financial model is perfect in the end.

All of which opens the door to rationalization, a seductive process by which we attempt to objectify that which we can't really know at its core. Anything can be rationalized. It's relatively easy, really. Debate teams do it all the time. They make a convincing and rational case for a position they themselves do not hold.

The modern executive is generally very good at rationalization. They have to be. Your ideas are worthless if you can't sell them to others. And nothing is more persuasive than a sound rationalization.

Instinct is generally considered to be inductive, since it emanates from the subconscious. I don't believe that makes it strictly subjective, however.

There is an article by Bryan Johnson, dated January 28, 2012, posted on listverse.com. (As I write this, it can be found at http://listverse.com/2012/01/28/top-10-human-reflexes-and-natural-instincts/.) He identifies the top ten human reflexes and natural instincts as follows:

1. Mammalian Diving Reflex—This reflex is triggered when cold water comes in contact with the face. It allows mammals to stay under water for extended periods of time. It maximizes oxygen output by slowing the heart rate and constricting blood flow to the extremities.
2. Vestibulo-Ocular Reflex—It allows you to move your head from side to side while focusing on the same visual image.
3. Yawning—We've all been there.
4. Emotional Contagion—Humans have a reflexive tendency to adopt the emotions of the people around them, believed to be the primary force behind mob psychology, which is alive and well in America today.
5. Cold Chills—They aren't triggered by the physical environment. They are a reflexive response to certain emotions.
6. Refractory Period—It has to do with sex. I won't go there.
7. Blushing—Try and stop it.
8. Knismesis and Gargalesis—These are fancy words for the effect of tickling.
9. Prisoner's Cinema—This refers to the light show people report seeing when confined to total darkness for long periods of time.
10. Post-Micturition Convulsion Syndrome—It is commonly known as a pee shiver.

A couple of observations: (1) They are universal to all people and (2) they are involuntary.

As such, can we really say that these instincts are subjective? They aren't a by-product of reason or analysis, and an individual's background or prior life experience has no bearing on their existence. Doesn't that, by definition, make these instincts about as objective as you can get?

So, I believe, is the instinct we classify as gut feel. It emanates from the subconscious, but that doesn't make it any less rational. Sure, intuition is influenced by past experience. But so is rational thought.

Subconscious conclusions, I believe, can be just as rational and objective as deductively reasoned ones. The only difference is our awareness of the mechanics of the process by which we reached a conclusion.

The former governor of New York, Mario Cuomo, said, "Every time I've done something that doesn't feel right, it's ended up not being right." After nearly four decades in the corporate trenches, I have to say that my own experience has been similar. My biggest bruises have come from self-inflicted punches after I rejected my gut instinct and failed.

Instinct is also a critical component of creativity. You can take a course in creative writing. But that won't make you a great novelist. And despite years of lessons as a child, the piano still eludes me. I can read music and tickle the keys, but I can't hear a tune and interpret it into song in the way that real musicians can.

In a similar vein, the process of visualization, which many athletes now use to improve performance, is really a process by which we attempt to internalize certain behaviors or actions to the level of instinct. There isn't time in the heat of competition to instruct the muscles in their every move. It must flow from the subconscious.

Instinct also helps to explain the value of experience and the learning curve, which states that the relationship between learning and practice is not linear. Experience, like visualization, allows us to internalize what we learn, recasting conscious thought as instinct. The impact on business can be profound.

Texas Instruments owned the early market for handheld calculators, but ultimately ceded the huge consumer market to Japanese manufacturers in part, many believe, because the company did not recognize the cost impact of the very steep learning curve that was to follow in the factories that made calculators. The Japanese competitors outpriced them by pricing their calculators at a level that would not satisfy current costs but were expected to cover the actual costs of production by the time the order was actually shipped.

Carla A. Woolf is a former CDA certified preschool teacher turned independent researcher and author. She notes, "Creativity does its best work when it functions intuitively..." It's a logical conclusion, actually.

Corporate executives are constantly on the hunt for out-of-the-box solutions to vexing problems. By definition that implies that simply extrapolating known or obvious solutions (i.e., rational solutions) won't do the trick. The best solution lies beyond the confines of reason.

Or do the truly best solutions just lie beyond the confines of conscious reason? Does reason demand preconceived consciousness? Even a superficial analysis of history would suggest not.

Do you think while you sleep? I do. Throughout my life many of my best ideas and solutions to problems were on the tip of my consciousness when I awoke in the morning. How did they get there? Any thoughtful process of problem solving is not obvious to me after the fact.

The reason this happens is because we loosen the reins of reason while we sleep. We apply a form of logic known as paralogic, which accommodates inconsistent arguments, leading to conclusions that are fallacious in the face of formal logic. The dreamt solution may not be viable or pragmatic, but that isn't automatic. What we initially assume to be fallacy may be the out-of-the-box solution we're seeking.

The converse, I believe, proves the point that induction, rather than deduction, is often the source of creative and effective solutions.

Carolyn Gregoire, senior writer for *Huffington Post*, has noted these two observations, among others, of highly intuitive people:

- They mindfully let go of negative emotions.
- They observe everything.

(huffingtonpost.com, March 19, 2014; updated April 28, 2015, available at http://www.huffingtonpost.com/2014/03/19/the-habits-of-highly-intu_n_4958778.html)

Both of these qualities, of course, contribute enormously to effective problem solving. The first fosters focus and eliminates potential bias. And the second—observation—is often the basis for deduction reason. Ironic that they are strengths of people who are inductively inclined, don't you think?

You might say that intuition and instinct are deductive logic that we simply can't articulate the reasoning behind. That doesn't mean it isn't true. It only means we can't explain it.

And since we can't explain the formal logic behind our creative solution, it is entirely possible that we got there by thinking less rigidly. Truth and reason, if we limit the latter to the formal logic of science and deduction, represent a false dilemma fallacy.

Can't a solution be valid and unreasonable at the same time? Don't children approach problem solving in a similar way? And don't we frequently associate childhood with creativity? Perhaps there is a very logical reason for that which lies just beyond the perimeter of the more structured analytical process we employ as adults.

Our instincts can be wrong, of course, which is why impulsive behavior can be reckless. And why it should be used with some restraint in the workplace, particularly as we acquire authority and our decisions have greater and greater impact.

So how do we know when to honor our instincts and when not to? That, I believe, is a matter of conscience. A component of the super-ego in Freud's model of psychoanalysis, conscience is the yardstick by which we calibrate right and wrong.

And since life often comes at us faster than we can digest, conscience is essential to the good and impactful life. All great leaders throughout history have shared a highly developed sense of conscience. From Mahatma Gandhi to Martin Luther King Jr. and Abraham Lincoln, conscience has been their inextinguishable guiding light.

The reason, I believe, is that conscience sits at the crossroad of deduction and induction. Some of it is naturally instinctive. And some of it is learned and acquired as we stumble through life.

The great American essayist, lecturer, poet, and leader of the transcendentalist movement, Ralph Waldo Emerson (1803–1882), wrote, "Trust instinct to the end, even though you can give no reason."

Sigmund Freud, on the other hand, noted, "It is impossible to overlook the extent to which civilization is built up upon a renunciation of instinct..." (*Civilization and Its Discontents*).

Both are correct. Together they define the sweet spot of reason.

For most but not all business leaders today that means learning to trust your instincts. There are times to trust the model prepared by the financial analysts, and there are times to trust your gut. And never trust the model if your gut doesn't concur until you can explain why you are comfortable with the answer, a precept to sound management covered in detail in chapter 28.

Or, as my mother used to say, "Everything in moderation."

Fifteen

Luck

In the West we attempt to define luck in objective terms. While we accept its intangibility, we often refer to it as a definable and distinct influence. We say, "Someone is watching out for me," or "Lady Luck is sitting on your shoulder," giving luck a very personal dimension.

The Chinese are very superstitious, which is the reason they like to gamble and are willing to pay extra for mobile-phone numbers that contain the number eight and do not contain the number four. (In China, you buy your mobile-phone number, and the cost varies depending on the superstition surrounding the numbers.)

Despite their proclivity for superstition, ironically, the Chinese define luck in very different terms than Westerners. Luck is not bestowed by a Supreme Being or mythical woman. It is more a case of good or bad fortune.

The distinction may seem trivial, but the nuance is significant. Luck is bestowed; fortune just is. Luck is supernatural; fortune is part of the natural order of the universe. You can facilitate good fortune or bad fortune, but it is not granted like a gift or a punishment in the way that good luck and bad luck are.

The nicest part about good fortune in the Chinese world view is that it can be shared. It can be passed along to others. It is not personal or individualized in the sense that Western luck is.

If you are playing craps at a casino in Las Vegas and the roller is hot, you may decide to bet with the roller. But you're still tagging along. In China, on the other hand, fortune belongs to the table. The roller may influence the fortune for good or bad, but the fortune that results is collective.

In China, the holiday of holidays is Spring Festival, known in the West as the Chinese New Year. In addition to launching the largest human migration on the planet as the Chinese return to their home-towns to celebrate with their extended families, it is a holiday typically filled with social interaction. People are out and about. (While restau-rants and retailers remain open, the country virtually shuts down.)

My favorite activity during Spring Festival was to attend one of the many Temple Fairs held around Beijing. Normally lasting five to six days, each Temple Fair had a slightly different personality but always offered a wide variety of regional foods and the chance to buy gifts and trinkets appropriate to the zodiac of the coming new year. Many also offered performances of traditional dance, song, drama, and comedy. And some offered games and rides much like you would find at an American carnival or old-style arcade.

During our first Spring Festival in China, my family attended our first Temple Fair, at which, of course, my daughters were imme-diately drawn to the rides and games. My youngest daughter, then four-years-old, wanted to play a carnival game of chance involving a large square table filled with small bowls, onto which the contestants launched a large plastic ball from about three feet away. The objective was to get the ball to come to rest in one of the few colored bowls, the color denoting which level of prize you won.

The bowl in the center of the table was the sole red bowl, red being the color of celebration and good fortune in China. If the ball rested there the contestant won a huge stuffed bear measuring three to four feet in length and two to three feet in width. While displayed prominently to lure customers, few were ever actually awarded. The odds were astronomically poor.

After waiting for a turn at the railing (like everywhere during Spring Festival, the fair was mobbed), the young attendant invited my daughter to stand on the railing around the perimeter to give her a fighting chance of even hitting the big table and keeping the ball on. Apparently concerned about getting the ball to the table, she gave the ball a mighty two-handed fling.

The ball landed on the table and bounced several feet in the air. I was sure it would quickly bounce off the table, as it often does, but in this case proceeded to bounce and bounce and bounce, before finally coming to rest in the red bowl in the middle.

You could hear a pin drop. Eyes sprung open, jaws dropped, and, after a moment's hesitation, a great cheer erupted. The Chinese, standing three or four deep on each side of the makeshift pavilion, leapt into the air cheering with all their might. You would have thought each of them had just won a crate of gold bullion. You couldn't help but be carried away in the genuine warmth and enthusiasm.

And why were they so ecstatic? Because a cute, little foreign girl with light-brown hair had won? No. They had all won. Good fortune had descended upon everyone present, the best of all possible omens that good luck would be with each of them in the coming new year.

My daughter's good fortune was a shared experience. Many, in fact, asked to have their picture taken with my daughter and her new bear, just to commemorate the event and insure that the good fortune clung to them in the coming year.

Imagine that same scene at an American carnival. Surely some would have been happy, even excited, to see the little girl win the teddy bear that was bigger than she was. (And which daddy had to carry for the rest of the day.) More than a few, I suspect, however, would walk away wishing, more than anything else, that *they* had been so lucky.

If you are a Westerner and travel to China with your family, you will surely have the experience of someone asking to have their picture taken with your children. My own daughters inevitably had their own not-so-little paparazzi whenever we ventured out to see the sights. I have pictures of them sitting on a curb at the Summer Palace eating an ice cream with a dozen or more people standing in front of them, all delightfully smiling and snapping away with their smartphones.

Most people who find themselves in that position assume that foreigners simply remain a relative novelty China. And there is some truth to that, certainly in the more rural areas. The real driving force, however, is the hope that the cute foreign children will bring good fortune to all.

Elderly men, in fact, often asked if they could touch my oldest daughter's hair, not because it was long, full, and wavy, but because it was the color of gold. And yes, it was a wee bit yucky, but they always asked first, and I always let them, and my daughter never minded. The optimism of good fortune finding us all was contagious.

The biggest limitation of Western notions of luck is that while we may readily acknowledge that good luck played a role in our successes, it's generally a tepid endorsement. And the reason is that if good luck is granted, what is bad luck? A withholding of good luck? Who wants to think that God is not watching over them but is watching over someone else? Who wants to think that Lady Luck likes the view from another's shoulder better than the view from yours?

In the Western view, luck is akin to a zero-sum game in gaming theory. If Lady Luck is riding on our shoulder, she can't be riding on the shoulder of the guy next to us. Luck, in other words, is all a bit competitive in the West.

Not so in China. The entire village can enjoy good fortune. Your good fortune does not come at anyone else's expense. It is very much a collectivist perspective.

In the American workplace, you seldom hear the language of luck. It doesn't fit in our deductive corporate world view. If a company is doing well, the quarterly press release will typically credit the results to good management, a sound strategy, or just sheer determination and hard work. Bad results, on the other hand, will probably be blamed on something completing external like the weather or the state of the economy.

In the hyperdeductive world of modern business, in other words, there is a tendency to shun luck and fortune. It's too intangible. It affronts our cultural and corporate senses of personal accountability and the supremacy of hard work.

This aversion to impersonal performance, however, blinds us to the voice of the inexplicable. We tune it out. We make every attempt to rationalize inexplicable events in a way that makes sense and acknowledges our deep held belief that we, as individuals, are at the center of the universe.

The reality, however, if we are willing to accept it, is that we aren't. We, as individuals, are not the nucleus around which the world turns. We can enhance the probability of success; we can certainly contribute to it. But there are a myriad of forces beyond our direct control that contribute to our success and failure, both individually and collectively.

In refuting that reality, in fact, we are contributing to our own disillusionment and, if not enhancing the chance of failure, precluding the pursuit of what may well be success. In failing to observe we are ignoring the many markers along the road that may, if observed and accepted, serve us well on our journey.

A singular focus on the logic of deduction will, in the end, deprive us of even greater success and may even fuel our failure. The universe simply does not function by deduction alone. Why should business be any different?

It is this singular focus, moreover, that fuels the angst, anxiety, and disillusionment so prevalent in the workplace today. Stress, as discussed elsewhere in the book, is not a function of pressure or an excessive workload. It is a direct result of the lack of control. We experience stress when we perceive that the task in front of us is beyond our knowledge, our skills, or the tools available to us.

When we personalize the performance of the organization, we inevitably personalize all performance of the individual. And this, inevitably, is where the stress comes in.

If your company rates personal performance on a scale of 1 to 5, with 5 being outstanding, you can rest assured that if the sales for your division come in below budget and you are the head of sales you won't be getting a 5. I guarantee it.

The best you can realistically hope for is a 3, and I've worked for bosses who would insist that under those circumstances you must, by definition, be rated a 1 or 2. That's where an exclusively deductive mind-set inevitably takes you.

You may deserve such a rating, of course. But you may not. Sales occur within the context of a larger competitive market, and that market exists within a larger economy. And sales are obviously influenced by the functionality, design, price, and quality of the product or service, none of which is within the control of the person ultimately closing the sale.

If you're beginning to think that I am against all personal accountability and assessment, I am not. I am an advocate for balance and perspective.

More specifically, I believe that we are the biographers of much of our angst and failure to achieve our desired goals. And it is all fueled by our exaggerated sense of personal influence and accountability. We simply give ourselves too much credit *and* too much blame, depending on the circumstances.

If we collectively step back and accept that we can sow the seeds of success and fortune but can't individually control it in most cases, our lives strike a greater sense of balance. Much of the stress dissipates. And, in fact, we enhance the chance that good fortune will befall all of us.

Sixteen

Individualism v. Collectivism

A merican culture and politics are built on a foundation of personal rights and freedoms. The right to vote, the right to bear arms, the right to practice our religion, and the right to trial by a jury of our peers are just a few of the rights that we have historically held dear.

It is an attractive social, political, and economic model that has served us well and helped to launch the American century. Our economy has prospered, our children have known opportunity, and our society, on balance, has flourished.

As the 2016 elections so indisputably revealed, however, the historically strong fabric of that individualistic model is beginning to fray. Entire segments of the population are feeling left behind and disenfranchised. And they have many very legitimate reasons to feel that way.

But what is the solution? To date, the segments of the population feeling the most threatened have sought to double down on the model of individual rights. For some this entails a rolling back, a return to the perceived days of law and order. For others, this requires a rolling out of additional legal protections to better reflect the composition of contemporary society.

Both remedies, however, are likely to fail because each, in its way, is an extreme solution that fails to define the problem in any greater context. Each requires a singular, one-dimensional perspective that

has, in fact, never existed. Neither solution is built on a factual interpretation of history.

I lived and worked in China from 2007 to 2016. Modern China, of
course, is built on a core Marxist philosophy. Officially they refer to it
as "socialism with Chinese characteristics."

Because Marxism and socialism are the conceptual opposites of
the rugged individualism that Americans hold dear, however, they are
political systems that are easily rejected out of hand by many in the
United States. Knee-jerk rejection by either side of the divide, however, seldom contributes to constructive dialogue and debate, so I
prefer to think in terms of individualism and collectivism. The former
focuses almost exclusively on the individual good promised by individual rights and freedoms, while the latter accepts that the collective
good must sometimes take precedent.

China's one child policy, officially known as the Family Planning
Policy, offers some insight. Implemented in 1979, it was the Chinese
government's solution to an exploding population that threatened to
destabilize social and economic order in the country.

I am married to a Chinese widow who was born prior to the imple-
mentation of the one child regulation. She was raised in a family of five
children, had ten aunts and uncles, and close to fifty cousins. When
she came of childbearing age, however, the one child policy was in
effect, and she was limited to having only one child, a boy now attending university in China.

American women are naturally appalled that government regulation can dictate family size. It is, to their way of thinking, a gross viola-
tion of individual rights and freedoms.

When I first asked my wife how she felt about the policy, however,
she was confused by the question. "Why would you ask that?" she
wondered. To her it was an issue unworthy of debate. The population was growing at an unsustainable rate. (The PRC had four hundred
thousand to five hundred thousand people in 1949, the year of its creation. It has close to 1.4 billion today, despite the introduction of the

one-child policy in 1979.) The government, she believes, had to do something in the interest of the collective good. And they did.

To her way of thinking, therefore, there is nothing to resent. And perhaps even less to waste time and energy debating. The government made the decision. Right or wrong is irrelevant. It is what it is.

Many Americans reading this tale will make summary and perhaps derogatory judgments about Chinese culture and politics. But that is unfortunate. It makes my previous point that a singular focus on individual rights and freedoms is ultimately exclusionary. As society marches along the continuum of political deduction, tilting the balance of power increasingly toward individual rights, somebody else ultimately suffers.

I would argue, moreover, that social progress has not conceded ground to the notion of individual rights but naturally pushed us further along the spectrum. Perhaps counterintuitively, this has, in the aggregate, compromised individual rights and freedoms at the same time.

Immigration is a good case in point. America is a nation of immigrants. Of that there can be no debate. My own ancestors, like the ancestors of every American other than Native Americans, came here from someplace else. Without immigration the shining city on the hill, as Ronald Reagan referred to it, would not exist.

Historically, however, the United States has been the land of assimilated immigration. The great melting pot was our signature to the world.

That is arguably less true today, a fact I make no case for or against. I understand it. But, more importantly, it is what it is. People understandably want to preserve their own cultures and language. I felt the same way for the time I lived in China.

Inevitably, however, there is less homogenization of cultural values and practices as a result. In attaining our individual cultural identity, we broaden the bandwidth of cultural norms and values, creating a greater likelihood that our individual rights and values conflict.

There is today a brewing debate on American university campuses over the traditional American value of free speech. Speakers who some find to be offensive in their beliefs are being denied the podium. It is a debate couched in terms of individual liberties and freedoms. Both sides, however, are arguing the same point. The only difference is perspective.

What's really missing from the debate is context. And as is often the case, context is where balance comes into play. Without context, the conflict cannot be resolved.

One missing piece of context, in this case, is the audience. Back when the Founding Fathers were debating the freedom of speech, that speech was pretty localized. An extremist of little notoriety might stand on a street corner and predict the end is near, but the audience and the impact was tiny. The position was not legitimized by the national stage.

That has all changed, of course. With the advent of social media and the 24-7 news cycle, there is little speech that doesn't have access to the national, even global, stage. And there are no real gatekeepers, as we have now learned, to protect the veracity of information that is widely disseminated.

And how do we resolve these conflicts? The simple answer is tolerance, but that in itself is a cultural value when it involves certain behaviors. No one has ever suggested that we be tolerant of terrorists or rapists. But those are the extremes, and there are plenty of behaviors and values where different people have different opinions. If we insist that only one opinion has merit, we cannot claim the high road of tolerance.

Of course, we can't resolve these conflicts through majority rule either. As the Founding Fathers clearly understood, a pure democracy in which majority rules opens the door to widespread exploitation of the minority by the majority.

Once again we're faced with the question: Do we need to compromise individual rights and values or add to them? That, however, is a deductive and singular solution that I think misses the point.

Individual rights cannot be assessed in isolation. Everything exists within a context. And the context that matters here is the degree to which we collectively agree to promote and protect the collectivist good.

I clearly don't have the individual right to commit murder. And while the simple reason is that it is both morally wrong and against the law, the contextual reason is that a society that condones murder cannot be a civil society. It cannot, in other words, be a society that exists for progress and justice.

Both assimilation (which, again, I don't necessarily advocate as I think it's an individual choice) and America's Judeo-Christian history have historically provided that collectivist context for American society to work within. In a society that puts great value on individual rights and freedoms, however, those individual rights and freedoms are destined to expand to the rhythm of our expanding universe.

In the past, American society achieved a certain sense of balance between individualism and collectivism through the broad acceptance of an absolute monotheistic moral code. That code, I would argue, is actually designed (By whom, you can decide for yourself.) to insure a proper balance between the individual and the community. And, I would add, between the logic of deduction and induction.

The fabric of that moral context, however, is fraying. In part, this is the natural path of social progression in a culture built on a foundation of deduction. As I have noted before, deduction feeds on itself, inevitably leading to more and more deduction, and that, in turn, inevitably leads to a greater and greater emphasis on the rights of the individual.

This march along the continuum of logic, however, is greatly accelerated by technology. Never before has the world been smaller. Never before has an individual been able to reach so many people in so little time and with so little cost and effort. It truly is mind-blowing.

I have traveled internationally throughout my four-decade career. And I clearly remember a day, not that long ago, when I could only stay in contact with my office and my family by telephone. And if you were calling from Hong Kong or Milan, for example, it wasn't cheap. As a result, international business travelers, certainly at my level, were inevitably out of touch for days at a time.

Even then, however, the world seemed to be shrinking at a very fast clip, largely due to the rapidly increasing convenience and rapidly decreasing cost of air travel. I recall many stories told by executives only one generation removed from me relating how easy my generational peers and I had it. They traveled exclusively by train and boat. And because we had been an international company from our earliest days, that often meant weeks, if not months, away from home and out of touch.

By the time I moved to China, however, that had all changed. In addition to e-mail, I had Skype, FaceTime, and WeChat. And, of course, video conferencing. I was never out of touch. I couldn't decompress from the stress of my work. While I worked for an American company, it had substantial operations in both the United States and Europe. If there was to be a global conference call, therefore, and there were many, the Asian team inevitably got the night duty. It's the only way the math of time zones will work. And because China's holiday calendar is decidedly different than the West's, and most Chinese holidays are unknown to most Americans, I could rest assured that I would be contacted for an urgent discussion while I was hiking the Great Wall in search of serenity and inspiration during the Mid-Autumn Festival.

That same technology now allows relatively small groups of people to spread their message far and wide. If the group is motivated and well funded enough, it can dominate both the news and the national dialogue to an extent far beyond the numerical significance of its membership.

And, once again, for every yin there is a yang. You no longer need to don a ski mask and acquire guns to rob a bank. You can rob an identity in your pajamas. And, of course, you can perpetrate falsehoods and innuendo far and wide while remaining protected by anonymity.

In short, technology does truly empower the individual. And, in many ways, that is a very good thing indeed. It facilitates social progress by giving the podium to all. It is, however, progress that is decidedly individualistic. While social media has the veneer of community, it is a community that is easily appropriated. There are no rules of governance.

It is the inevitable absoluteness of deduction that gives us such extreme individual rights. But that isn't quite accurate. It is the existence of deduction in isolation that gives us those extremes. It is the absence of the balancing power of induction that allows the individual, in whatever way, good or bad, to reign over the larger community in which we live and work.

Chinese culture is far more collective in scope and practice than Western culture. And, perhaps not surprisingly, the Internet is highly regulated there. There is no pornography. Fake news, although that is often in the eye of the beholder, is promptly removed. Netizens are legally held accountable for what they say and the rumors they spread.

On balance, I heard few Chinese complain about government censorship while I was there. There are exceptions, of course. As inductivists, however, there is a greater willingness to accept reality without judgment. It is what it is.

To be clear, I am not advocating we move in the direction of government censorship. There are pros and cons to everything. And sometimes the risks of the cons outweigh the penalties of the pros.

The Chinese are fighting the same battle to achieve balance between the rights of the individual and the rights of the community as we are. They are just coming from the other direction. The difference is that they accept the need for balance. They accept that nothing exists in isolation. The individual, like it or not, exists within the context of the collective. Our rights, both within the workplace and within society at large, should promote balance between the two.

Seventeen

The Vision Thing

After graduating from college, I took a job with a well-known multi-national company with a long and highly respected legacy. Nearly all of the senior executives had started their careers following World War II and had been with the company their entire career. And nearly all had risen through the ranks of a single department.

Not long after my arrival, there was a transition of power in the C-suite when the current CEO, the grandson of the company's founder, retired. It was an orderly transition. The new CEO, as was commonplace at the time, had also worked at the company for most of his career and had been the heir-apparent for some time. Nobody batted an eye.

Soon after moving into the corner office, he made the public observation that virtually all department heads had only worked in their current department throughout their decades of tenure. That, he suggested, needed to change. The executive of the future, he wisely reasoned, needed a functionally diverse skill set and lens on the business.

To that end, he and the senior leadership team undertook what would today be called a succession-planning exercise. Some might call it "mapping the future talent." They identified the young peo-ple in the organization whom they believed had the most promise to become the future leaders of the company when the post–World War II generation ultimately retired, a changing of the guard that would occur over a relatively short period of time. And I had the good fortune to be on the list.

The senior leadership team then worked with each of the employees to develop a professional development plan with the objective of giving each a diverse functional experience in the company. To management's credit, the employee was very much a part of this exercise. In my case, I was eventually given three scenarios and allowed to pick the one that appealed to me most.

There were, of course, pros and cons to everything, even back then. The potential con of a development program of this type, sometimes formally labeled as a management training program (our CEO, to his credit, refused to label the program), is that an employee typically knows exactly how long he or she is to remain in his or her current position and may not, therefore, make sound long-term decisions. The other big con, of course, is that when you identify who is on the list, you potentially demotivate those who are not.

To overcome that pitfall, our assignments were open ended. We went into our new assignments accepting that we might spend the rest of our career there if we didn't continue to perform up to expectations. And we all got the message.

The members of the group, of course, fully understood, without being told, that the other members of the group were our primary competition for future advancement. There would never be more than one CEO.

Today that would probably lead to a drama not unlike occurs on the once popular reality show, *Survivor*. In that contest the most effective strategy for moving on is not to outperform the other contestants but to be part of an alliance that votes some other contestant off. It's a terrible life lesson, really, and not one I want my own daughters to mimic. (Also the reason the Founding Fathers were wary of pure democracy, by the way.)

Nonetheless, our team did not adopt this strategy. We believed that the game would be fair and that we each had a spot, if not the spot, on the team of the future. The challenge would be decided, we all trusted, on the basis of merit.

In our case, therefore, rather than adopting the *Survivor* mentality we adopted a strategy similar to the one used by cycling teams in the Tour de France. While we didn't have a team leader per se, we worked together. We supported each other. And we did so because we knew that the contest that mattered most was the company's growth and success. The more successful the company was, the greater the chance that each would find a fulfilling career, even if we couldn't all be the CEO.

While we did eagerly and voluntarily spend a lot of time together, both socially and on the job, we didn't team off. We never identified as team members, and we actively recruited new members on our own. We knew that solving the biggest problems would take broad collaboration, although we referred to it as simply working together in those days.

On one such occasion, a group of us were sitting around after work one day discussing the perceived need for the company to have a mission statement to guide its efforts. Mission statements were all the rage at the time, and we didn't have one.

Part way through the discussion the CEO walked in, his ever-present pipe in mouth and suit coat on and buttoned. He cheerfully asked us what we were discussing and when we told him, he bit down on his pipe, and his body language made it clear that he had lost his cheer.

He then said, in no uncertain terms, "Our mission is to pay the god damn bills. That's all anyone needs to know."

That, actually, isn't so bad for a mission statement. It's actionable. It's clear. And, most importantly, it states both what we are and what we aren't. It sets priorities.

In contrast, here are a few mission statements from an article written by Minda Zetlin, published by *Inc.* on November 15, 2013, entitled "The 9 Worst Mission Statements of All Time":

- To create a shopping experience that pleases our customers, a workplace that creates opportunities and a great working environment for our associates, and a business that achieves financial success.
- To help make every brand more inspiring, and the world more intelligent.
- [Company name] is the leader in entertainment & hospitality— a diverse collection of extraordinary people, distinctive brands, and best in class destinations.
- Continuing (founder's name) legacy of commitment to consumers, community, and children, we provide high-quality (company's name) products while conducting our business in a socially responsible and environmentally sustainable manner.

I've eliminated the companies' names only because I think it's unfair to single out these four companies. In reality, the list of horrible corporate mission statements would fill a dictionary-sized tome.

The first mission statement, of course, fails to identify who the target customers are. The second one seems a bit grandiose for a company that makes things like labels and binder dividers. The third documents the current state but doesn't have a whiff of aspiration. The fourth is not bad but remains a little broad to be of real value. What doesn't it commit to?

To have any real value, a mission statement should be both an elevator speech to customers and investors and a guiding light that employees can reference in their day-to-day activities. Admittedly, that's not easy to do. It's akin to writing a tweet that's worthy of anyone's time, but you can get pretty close.

That it has to be concise and use words that people actually understand goes without saying. What really matters, however, is that it is actionable, and, most importantly, it sets priorities. It's not enough to tell people what's important. You must tell them what is of less importance.

Setting priorities is particularly important one level down from the mission statement, in the long-range plan, or what some companies call the strategic plan. This should give some substance to the mission, but it won't if it doesn't establish real priorities.

Frankly, I've yet to see a great one. (I've yet to see a Northern Hairy Nose Wombat, either, but that doesn't mean they don't exist.) And most fall short because they try to be all things to all people.

I have worked on several long-range plans over the course of my career. And I've worked with some of the best consultants in the business. In the end we were generally happy with the finished product and were able to conceptualize it into a cute little graphical form that could be plastered on posters and tent cards.

Without exception, however, we inevitably gave something to every functional area represented on the team that developed the strategy. There were key initiatives for HR, engineering, sales, marketing, accounting, and finance. No one was ever left out.

That, of course, diluted the priorities. And, in some ways, it killed any potential collaboration because ever function had its own objective of strategic importance, and those objectives could be mutually exclusive.

What ultimately doomed the plan, however, was the passage of time. And the window typically wasn't open very long. Things changed, everybody reacted, and the posters yellowed.

This is why I've come to believe that mission statements and long-range plans are largely a waste of time. Somebody needs to be thinking about the future. And some departments, like the engineering department in a capital-intensive industry, need to be working on a fairly long horizon. Taken in the proper context, however, those don't need to be massive projects involving every functional constituency of the company.

I do think that the most productive way to achieve the past objectives of the mission statement and the long-range plan is to develop a list of the company's core values. But, and it's a big but, they must be actionable and they must establish clear and sincere priorities.

Steve Jobs is famously quoted as saying that the founders of Apple did not set out to build the world's best PC. They set out, "To put a dent in the universe." I don't know if he said it or in what context, but I think it's a great inspiration and guiding light. Here's what it says:

- We want to be audacious in our goals and objectives.
- Good is not good enough.
- Creativity is valued here.
- The technology is secondary to its impact.
- We want to put our effort and investment where it will make a difference.
- We're different and we like it that way.
- We want to be the first in whatever we do.
- We want to do things we can tell our grandkids about.
- We want to be disruptive.
- We want people to know who we are.

And I could go on. A timeless, fully informative agenda in just seven words.

Apple went on to become the first US corporation to be valued above $700 billion. That's billions. And that's a big dent.

The key to this vision is that it is entirely inductive. It addresses the what and the why. It makes no attempt to address the how, except in general terms and by inference.

The mistake most companies make in defining their future is that they try to describe it in the language of deduction. It's just another example of the corporate fixation on the tangible language of how.

Compare Jobs's vision to the four mission statements referenced in the beginning of this chapter.

In the first mission statement, the key words are, "pleases," "opportunities," and "achieves." Those are all things you do or create. The emphasis is on doing.

In the second mission statement, the key words are "inspiring" and "intelligent." But the phrase that hijacks the mission is "to help make."

The third mission statement isn't even a vision. It's a metric of the perceived current state. And it's a bit self-congratulatory for my tastes.

The fourth mission statement, the best of the group, finally introduces the language of induction. The company is committed and responsible.

The language of deduction is seductive (an inductive word) because it is considered to be more objective, less wishy-washy. That, however, is largely a myth of perception.

Go back to Steve Jobs's vision. A "dent" is pretty inductive, but we can easily visualize it. As is "universe." A mental image quickly comes to mind.

Once again we are reminded of the imprecise nature of language itself. In the extreme, everything folds back into its opposite. Deductive becomes inductive; inductive becomes deductive.

So don't get hung up on the words themselves. What is the message? Is it clear? Is it concise? Does it provide guidance for behavior? And, of course, is it worthy?

Chances are that the message you want is living at the junction of induction and deduction, not at either extreme. Induction defines the goal. Deduction provides the how. And both together define the why. Of the three, the why, as discussed in chapter 10, is the most critical. That's what gives employees, customers, and investors alike the aspiration that is behind all true motivation and dedication.

Eighteen

Youth

As noted throughout history, the children are our future. They will eventually inherit the reins of power and define our society.

What we define as the maturing process, however, is often a process of assimilation. The young get older, their priorities change, and they generally adopt values and behaviors more in line with their parents.

That does not mean our children will follow robotically in our footsteps, however. Each generation evaluates previous values and norms through a new lens. They become the agents of change, however incremental, abolishing negative stereotypes, myopic thinking, and the worst aspects of past social injustice.

When I worked in China, I was the only employee over the age of fifty in a company of more than three hundred. And I benefited greatly from that. The Chinese have great respect and admiration for their elders. They view them as a source of knowledge and experience, and respect for the elderly is a valued Chinese tradition that is uniformly embraced.

That was a very pleasant change for me at the time. For much of my own career, American business has been smitten with youth. That was great, of course, when I was young and full of piss and vinegar, as my mother used to put it. It lost its luster, however, as I got older. People like Bill Gates and Warren Buffett still have a lot of influence, but youth continues to be a decidedly prized commodity among corporate boards and investors.

There are many theories as to why, but I think the reason is largely one of logic. Young people tend to be more inductive in their world view. Induction is the logic of dreams and aspirations. As we age, however, we naturally become more deductive in our world view. Experience starts to bog us down, and our dreams, in many cases, start to seem just beyond our reach.

If the people running a business become exceedingly inductive in their world view, in other words, as the young bucks returning from World War II may have been so inclined, organizations will naturally seek leaders with the deductive perspective that comes from experience to steady the helm. And if the leaders become excessively deductive, there will be a natural inclination to search out leaders with the naturally inductive world view of youth and the ability to challenge existing paradigms and think outside the proverbial box.

That is, of course, exactly what happened when technology became so disruptive to American commerce back in the '90s. Many experienced but deductive leaders were caught flatfooted. It wasn't a deductive revolution, and they didn't see it coming. The young took over. They were more inductive in their world view, and they saw what was happening much more clearly. They could more easily adapt.

Like most models, however, the model of experience and logic is not static. Nor does it exist in isolation. There are often many cyclical oscillations occurring concurrently.

As in most Western societies, the youth of China are beginning to move away from the values and behaviors of their parents. Some of their elders, of course, as they do elsewhere, lament the change.

In the case of the Chinese, that movement is one of departure from the largely inductive foundation of traditional Chinese culture. The move is incremental, for sure, but the youth of China are inclined to be less superstitious and to more willingly embrace notions of individual values and freedoms than their collectively minded parents.

In the United States, on the other hand, our youth appear to be migrating toward a more inductive world view, as discussed in chapter 6, rejecting many of the deductive values of their parents. On balance, I believe this is a good thing and just further evidence of the sine wavy theory behind the rhythms of the universe.

But is this social progress or does social change simply move along the universal sine wave? The answer is both.

Social futurists are often wrong. And they are wrong, more often than not, because their projections are simply out of phase. Perhaps they extrapolate the past with a ruler, when French curve might be more appropriate. Or perhaps they are Promethean at a time when the world is moving deliberately along a predictable continuum.

In the early '90s, I was managing the retail division of a well-known consumer-products company. And in that role, I felt it appropriate to think a great deal about the future. So I did, and I shared my predictions in a pamphlet designed to build some context to guide our future product development and marketing efforts.

I don't honestly remember all of my predictions, but I do remember one of them very clearly because I was spectacularly wrong. I could not have been more wrong, in fact. I predicted, with a very high degree of confidence, that the tattoo would soon disappear from the American body.

My logic, of course, was deductively logical. The same cultural pioneers who got married barefoot in the '60s and '70s were becoming increasingly conscious of their health and fitness. The body was the new temple. Everyone was getting colonics, drinking carrot juice, joining health clubs, and learning to meditate. In that frame of mind, why would anyone get a tattoo?

Faith Popcorn, the renowned futurist, was concurrently predicting the rise of cocooning, a home furnishings trend wherein boomers put more and more of their money into decorating and securing their homes in an effort to build a refuge from the feverish and unsettled world around them. It was an inductive prediction at the time, and she was right. Home entertainment became more commonplace, and companies like Crate & Barrel emerged as the darlings of the retail industry.

But what are the millennials doing? They're moving back downtown into smaller and less isolated spaces, meeting friends at bars and clubs, and generally pursuing social lives built around shared experiences.

In retrospect, I was too deductive in predicting the demise of the tattoo. I was out of phase. As it turned out, more than half of the US population now has one or more tattoos, and many have turned the tattoo into a lifestyle.

The antiwar protests of the 1960s were all about rejecting the globalism of the political and corporate establishment of the time. Our parents had fought in World War II and were both patriotic and accepting of broad, vaguely defined political goals like stopping the spread of communism.

My generation saw the body bags on the nightly news and wanted to know why. We wanted a logical explanation for why we should put our lives on the line in the jungles of an undeveloped country on the other side of the globe. There was no Hitler or Pearl Harbor to rally around. We only saw red arrows on a map, and it wasn't compelling imagery.

It is that same generation, however, that has gone on to become the globalists of today. A September 2015 article in *The Nation*, written by Nick Turse, managing editor of TomDispatch.com and a fellow at The Nation Institute, noted that US Special Operations forces had already deployed to 135 nations in the first nine months of 2015. These elite troops, he went on, were carrying out eighty to ninety missions each and every day all across the globe.

Our children, of course, are now questioning our globalist model. But for very different reasons than we questioned the Vietnam War. We deduced our way into fighting the establishment in place at the time; the millennials are inducing their way into fighting us.

We deduced our way into Iraq and Afghanistan, and we deduced our way into a new paradigm of tight immigration control. Our youth, however, are increasingly embracing the inductive values of inclusion and the elimination of both privilege and conspicuous consumerism.

In this way I believe our children are more like the greatest generation than they are like their parents. Both the greatest generation and the millennial generation were and are decidedly inductive in their world view. The two generational views differ greatly, in some cases markedly, but both share a highly inductive embrace of ennobled ideals and values, while the generations between them enclasped the deductive tools of commerce and global trade.

There are, as always, a couple of caveats to the natural sine rhythm of induction and deduction. And they're important, but they don't negate the reality of the oscillations. They merely impact the wavelength of those oscillations.

The first caveat is that we tend to naturally migrate toward deduction as we get older. Experience is the fuel of deduction. The more we experience in life the more we are prone to deduce predictions and conclusions.

The second is that traumatic world events tend to instill inductive values. My parents had World War II. My daughters have…well, take your pick. In each case world events have given us a reason to pause and take stock.

This brings us to the third caveat. Deduction is easier to defend. The language of deduction is simply more powerful because it is more tangible and finite. As noted previously, the inductive world view requires a certain leap of faith that can be difficult to sustain in the face of deductive argument, particularly if the argument is a false dilemma fallacy.

Deductive conclusions are difficult to argue your way around. You often have to reach the point where enough is enough, and you simply reject the deduction as a matter of principle. And since principles aren't always easy to grasp, and even harder to hold on to, it sometimes takes a while to make the turn.

I believe it is clear, however, that the United States is making that turn. Our youth of today will leave a decidedly inductive mark on American culture. They may have acquired the inductive world view of their grandparents, but the deductive obstinacy of their boomer parents.

American business must take note. Many of our current corporate leaders are decidedly out of step with their youngest customers and employees. And those two groups are only going to get bigger. Eventually, of course, they will seize power. The only question is how painful the transition will be?

To minimize the tumult, corporate leaders must temper the relentless march toward deduction and begin once again to embrace values and ideals rather than financial models, forced bell curves, the growing polarization of pay scales, the deductive but hollow marketing plan, the forced servitude of the 24-7 electronic collar, and the empty promise of shared destiny.

Instead we must promote the values of true inclusion and diversity, the behavior of integrity, and the commitment of true obligation. We must treat each and every member of the organization with respect and the unshakable optimism that they can and will do a good job. We must stop pulling from the top and learn to support from behind. Only then, in the sweet spot between deduction and induction, will we realize the true potential of our people and the organizations they collectively define.

Nineteen

Building an Organization

Most books on organization will tell you to define the ideal organization first and to fill in the names second. I disagree. I think you should start with the list of names and then draw the lines.

The latter approach, of course, is more inductive than the first, but that shouldn't surprise you by now. I do, however, have some very deductive reasons for my preference.

"Does Anybody Really Know What Time It Is?" was a 1969 hit song written by Robert Lamm, a member of the iconic rock band Chicago. It was ultimately released as a single and became a top ten record, peaking at #7.

A similar question, I believe, is "Does anyone really know who you are?" Your mother probably comes closest. And hopefully your spouse or partner is up there in the top five. In the end, however, only you and your God, if you believe in one, know all of the details.

Your boss doesn't. And in some cases, your boss knows next to nothing about you. The HR director probably doesn't either. And chances are that the peers and subordinates who contribute to your 360-degree review only know the parts of you that you've opened to the public. And that's typically not much.

Titles and job descriptions, moreover, are not all-inclusive. And they are open to interpretation. The job description for a chief marketing officer is pretty consistent from one company to the next. The actual role played by the individual assigned that title, however, is as varied as the individuals and the companies themselves. No two are identical.

This is one of the reasons why building an organization around the job description is generally a mistake. It doesn't define the role you want the individual to play. And that role, in the every-changing world business operates in, will inevitably change over time.

Because your knowledge of a person is typically superficial, of course, there is no way to be absolutely sure that you've built the right box around them when you employ the method I advocate. Your chances, however, are greatly enhanced. And the methodology itself suggests that it's no big deal if you find the organization needs some tweaking along the way.

The world is a dynamic place. Business is just a microcosm of those dynamics. In the end, all business must continually adapt to changing circumstances. And you can do that proactively or at the pointed end of the figurative sword.

The traditional method for building an organization is really just another form of pigeonholing, a decidedly deductive process in my mind. Whether or not you are going to the extreme of trying to force a square peg into a round hole, the fit is never perfect. And while that may be good enough for some, the greatest companies strive for perfection. They never achieve it, and don't expect to. But the company that puts up the best fight, not the acceptable fight, inevitably wins the war.

Early in my career, I was invited to tour the Sikorsky Aircraft helicopter plant in Stratford, Connecticut. I don't remember how I got invited, since I've never worked in any related industry, but beyond the size and impressive organization of the plant, there are two things I remember vividly about that trip.

The first is a total digression. But there's a place for levity in every conversation.

I flew into a small local airport on a regional airline that surely doesn't exist anymore. The plane was a twin-prop propeller plane that held six to eight passengers. And when I walked out on the tarmac to board, there was the pilot pouring a can of oil into one of the engines. Spout and all, just as in a traditional gas station.

On the way home late that afternoon, the plane was similar, if not the same one I had flown in on that morning. And while there were no cans of oil in sight, once we took off, the copilot turned around and shouted (it was pretty noisy), "There's a cooler of pony beers under the last seat there if the gentleman sitting there wouldn't mind passing them around." And he did, and we all took one. How could you not?

The most memorable part of that trip, however, was the business card my host handed me upon my arrival. I don't remember his name, but I do remember his title. He was the manager, factory of the future. And, as you would always hope, but not always find, he had a personality that fit the title like hand in glove.

I got it. I immediately knew what this guy did, and I had a pretty good idea as to how he fit into the organization and the role he was expected to play. A manager, special projects, or VP, manufacturing, title would have been far less informative.

As a rule, I've always been pretty lenient with the titles of the people who work for me. In fact, I've even put a policy in place to disallow titles, with a few exceptions, to be printed on business cards, although that was more of an attempt to save money than to signal any specific organizational philosophy. A lot of business cards end up in the landfill simply because someone got a new title, everything else remaining the same.

Most people who want to contact you after an initial introduction don't really care so much about your title unless you are in the C-suite. They will assess your role largely based on the impression you gave when you met. Or they just want an in, and the department you work in is enough information to know if you might be able to help.

I have actually toyed with the idea of letting everyone define his or her own title, but I've never quite had the courage to pull the trigger. I always thought that would tell me more about the person than any formal or informal attempt to assess them. If anyone chose the title of emperor or king, for example, I would know to call security immediately. No need to waste any more time.

In Chinese there are very few words that translate literally into English. Mandarin is more a language of images and notions than finite nouns, adjectives, or verbs. And since Mandarin does not use the Roman alphabet (Pinyin, a proxy for Mandarin that uses the Roman alphabet, also uses four tones that distance it from written English), a Chinese speaker actually shapes his mouth and uses his tongue in ways that differ from a native English speaker.

Many Chinese names, therefore, are difficult for Americans to pronounce. As a result, nearly all Chinese who expect to communicate with a native English speaker, either professionally or personally, assign themselves an English name. And unless their Chinese name is one of the few that has a literal translation, or there is a name that is phonetically similar, you can pick any name you want. It has no legal status, so have some fun.

So if you go to China, you will probably meet Brenda, Susan, and Kevin. But you might also meet Sun, Sky, and Summer. And, yes, I found, on balance, that the taken names fit pretty well.

But back to organizations and titles. In addition to allowing people to define their own title, I've often wondered if it didn't make sense to reshuffle the teams every few years by allowing the top managers to reselect their teams from the bottom up as we used to do in gym class when I was a kid. (I understand that most schools no longer allow captains to choose their teams. Teams have to be assigned randomly, which may avoid hurt feelings, but may promote gambling once kids realize that teams can be strong or weak depending on how the dice are rolling—that LOUC thing.)

To avoid complete chaos, you could employ a system not unlike that used by the NFL or NBA. That would give you some continuity but allow each team to customize the roster to the specific needs and operating style of that particular team. And it would obviously be a great incentive to always perform at your best or to reach beyond your best if you actually wanted to be traded.

However you define your organization, don't get carried away by the process. In the end, the quality of the players and the quality of the coaching will mean far more than how the boxes are connected. You have to have a structure. Just make sure that structure is built around the right parameters. You're not solving an equation; you're building a team.

Twenty

The Rule of Law

The United States is a nation of laws upheld by an independent judiciary. Businesses and individuals alike are expected and ultimately forced, with some notable exceptions, to operate within their boundaries.

As the US economy and culture have become more complex, however, so too have the laws and regulations that seek to influence our behaviors. This has had several consequences for American business.

The first is that our laws and regulations have expanded exponentially in an effort to keep up with the complexity of the behaviors they seek to influence. The birth and blistering growth of the Internet provides just one example.

Leonard Kleinrock is the UCLA professor credited with sending the first message through a packet switcher, now called a router, in 1969. That network ultimately became the World Wide Web. And with the help of millions of people, according to Kleinrock in an interview with CNN in 2009, the Internet was born.

In that same interview with Philip Rosenbaum, however, Kleinrock admitted that Internet pioneers did not fully consider the potential dark side. According to David D. Clark, an MIT scientist with the nickname "Albus Dumbledore," the threat only became obvious some twenty years later, in 1988, with the introduction of the first malevolent computer worm, ultimately dubbed the Morris Worm, named after the Cornell University graduate who created it.

Echoing this sentiment, according to a 2015 article in *Washington Post* by Craig Timberg, fellow pioneer Vinton G. Cerf conceded, "We didn't focus on how you could wreck this system intentionally."

But the law of unintended consequence is both timeless and universal. And its dark implications expand rapidly with complexity. The more complex our world becomes, the darker its potential, as current world events clearly bear out.

The law cannot keep pace. It is constrained by the reality that language is a simplified variation of reality designed to facilitate efficient communication. The more complex our laws and regulations become, the more opportunity there is to skirt them and to find the loopholes buried within.

The United States and China come at the rule of law from opposite directions and the comparison is illuminating.

In the US civil and regulatory justice systems, guilt and innocence turn on words. Legislatures pass expansive laws laid out in great detail. They must address every possible application of the law and its exceptions. If they don't a plaintiff or defendant with a good lawyer will drive right through the loophole.

The *Federal Register*, the federal government's daily report of proposed and actual changes to rules and regulations, notices, and presidential documents, was 2,620 pages long in 1936, the first year it was published. By 2015 the number of pages had ballooned to roughly eighty-two thousand. And, of course, the more words written, the more the lawyers have to argue over.

In China, by contrast, the judiciary is in its infancy and has only recently been given independence from the political arm of government, and there is very little in the way of case law, the foundation of the Western legal doctrine of precedence. And the regulations and laws themselves are extremely vague, allowing government officials wide latitude in interpreting and applying them.

On the positive side of the ledger, this provides local government officials in China the flexibility to adapt laws and regulations to local needs and circumstances. No lawyer or lawmaker could ever articulate every possible application of the legislation they are attempting to commit to paper, so this flexibility does have a lot of merit in a country as big and diverse as China. On the other hand, it does open the door to rogue government behavior and can potentially impede Beijing's ability to implement national policy.

In effect, the American legal system is built on a foundation of deduction that starts with the rights of citizens and corporations and builds on them to establish government authority. The Chinese legal system, on the other hand, is inductive, starting with government authority and exercising that to establish the rights of the individual. The former turns on a conceptual framework of individualism, while the latter turns on a conceptual framework of collectivism.

Both countries are moving to the middle, the sweet spot of logic, the balance of deduction and induction. In the case of the Chinese, they are consciously promoting individual rights through legal reform aimed at increasing the independence of the judiciary. The United States, on the other hand, is actively seeking to promote collective rights through increased regulation and ever more expansive laws that strengthen the hand of the government. (This battle between the competing philosophies of individualism and collectivism, of course, is at the heart of the political division we experienced in the 2016 elections and continue to witness as I write this.)

As the United States introduces more and more laws and regulations, of course, the greater the power of the judges and juries who interpret those laws and regulations. And while the judiciary is itself an institution, it is staffed with individuals who can no more escape their humanity, and the natural tendency to interpret reality through their own world view, than the rest of us. So while the individualists among us decry the perceived subversion of activist judges, it is really the legislative and administrative branches of government who have enabled them through laws and regulations.

As noted throughout this book, deductive systems are self-motivating. They feed on themselves and inevitably introduce more and more deduction. Inductive systems, on the other hand, are self-perpetuating. They tend to stay where they are. Which is why China will face many challenges in its efforts to move toward the Western legal model and why the United States will continue to experience severe pushback from those who want to contain the power of the judiciary.

For American business, this more activist legal system, in conjunction with the sweeping and instantaneous reach of social media and the "condemn from a distance" culture it empowers, the growing polarity in wealth, and the growing divide in education and opportunity, has created a perfect storm of immense risk. And it is a risk that corporate officers and the board of directors are increasingly held personally accountable for, greatly enhancing their incentive to actively manage it.

At a time when risks are escalating, the tools of subversion are likewise becoming more and more powerful. Pharmaceutical companies live in constant fear that someone will secretly taint their products. Banks fear that their computer networks will be hacked. Airlines fear that terrorists will utilize their planes to inflict death.

Investors have reacted to this rapid expansion of risk, in part, by demanding that the companies they invest in step up their game in relation to managing risk. And business leaders have largely complied. Most companies now take great pains to identify risks, manage them, and insure against potential losses. To the point where food companies often try to break into their own facilities and virtually every company with a network is hiring specialized security firms to try and hack their systems to expose vulnerabilities. And if all else fails, there are legions of crisis consultants to guide you through the aftermath.

Risk management, however, is inevitably subject to the law of diminishing returns. The spectrum of risk is infinite. It can never be fully eliminated. There are simply too many variations of risk, many unseen at the moment, to protect against them all. At some point along the spectrum, the cost of protection outweighs the likely impact of the risk itself.

Much of American business, I believe, has crossed that threshold. Companies are draining their scarce financial resources, stifling innovation, and demoralizing the organization that ultimately has to live with the red tape and bureaucracy. And, of course, the cost of the people who are assigned the task of managing risk, usually the legal or finance department, are just the tip of the iceberg when it comes to measuring the true costs of risk management.

As the general manager of a Chinese subsidiary of an American company, I spent a lot of time and effort implementing and supporting corporate systems designed to minimize risk. I had to watch online videos detailing the requirements of the Foreign Corrupt Practices Act (FCPA), populate generic spreadsheets attempting to quantify the risks we faced for the board of directors, and managing administrative and legal systems designed to insure customers and suppliers were aware of the restrictions of the FCPA and were, in fact, in compliance. Suffice it to say we killed a forest of trees annually.

I put no blame on the legal department. Our lead counsel is a friend and one of the smartest people I know. She is simply doing the job that our deductive legal and regulatory system has put on her plate. The problem is not activist corporate counsel any more than we can blame our displeasure with the state of the law in the United States on activist judges. If we need to blame someone or something, we need look no further than the logic of deduction.

There is another by-product of legal deduction that further accelerates the march along the continuum of deduction to its inevitable activist conclusion. It is the special interest group.

In a deductive legal system, the people who write the laws and the courts that uphold them drive outcome. The deductive rule of law itself, therefore, creates a fertile environment for special interest groups to wield their financial and voting power in an effort to influence politicians and the regulatory apparatus—the people and institutions that author and manage the rules and regulations of the deductive state.

The scope of their existence and efforts, not surprisingly given the deductive nature of our legal system, is fairly narrowly defined. They exist to protect the rights of the LGBT community, gun owners, the environment, women, people of color, and so on and so on. They don't exist to promote social equity of *all* kinds, fairness to *all* people, or the rights of *all* communities. Those are inductive notions.

People, of course, are less likely to provide as much financial support to institutions that support broad inductive rights rather than the specific, deductive rights that is the focus of special interest groups today. But that is a conclusive backhanded way to prove that if we really want to take the money out of politics, the solution is not to create more deductive rules and regulations. As past efforts at campaign finance reform have conclusively shown, there will always be a way around deductive rules and regulations.

If we really want to take the money out of politics, more regulation of the political process is not the answer. The answer is to adapt a more inductive world view among the citizenry and the political and legal institutions that serve it. More deduction will only lead to more division.

It is deduction, moreover, that is crippling small business and generally constricting employment of wage growth. The effectiveness of deductive tools comes at a steep price in terms of complexity and the cost of compliance.

That doesn't mean, however, that there should be less regulative intent or that we should compromise collective rights in the name of individual rights. It does mean changing the focus and intent of that regulation. It means promoting the tools and rights of induction. It means finding the equilibrium, the sweet spot, between the rights and ideals of the individual and society at large.

Twenty-One

Optimism

All great leaders are genuinely optimistic. From Martin Luther King Jr. to Ronald Reagan, they get up each day expecting good things to happen. They have dreams, and they are confident that those dreams can be achieved.

Optimism is all about faith and hope. It is an inductive mind-set that isn't built on a platform of reasons and causes. It just is. It is simple, and it is productive. Optimism begets optimism. It is a more expansive form of precognitive conclusion. If we believe something good can happen, it often does.

Pessimism, on the other hand, is a deductive mind-set built on a more detailed analysis of what could go wrong. It is built on a platform of dissection and analysis that hope cannot overcome. It is expansive in scope but narrow and one-dimensional in its focus—failure.

Optimism is critical to the nurturing of a healthy, productive, and effective organization. When the culture and leadership of an organization is pessimistic, the employees get by. When it is optimistic, they move mountains.

Pessimism is both self-fulfilling and transparent. If you are pessimistic that one of your employees can perform a task or role, they will certainly sense your lack of faith, no matter what lengths you go to hide it. And they will, knowingly or not, probably oblige your expectations.

The same is true in parenting. My greatest moments of pride in my daughters have, without exception, come at the times of my greatest optimism as a parent. Not because that instilled in my daughters a desire to please me, but because it pushed open the door to success in their own minds. It allowed them to believe.

Much of the great strength of optimism comes from the simple fact that it is far more efficient than pessimism. If you can make the leap of faith to optimism, it eliminates all of the worry and angst required to fuel and sustain pessimism. You start the journey further down the trail.

Because so many of the tools of modern business are built around the concepts of planning and control, risk management, and cost containment, it is often difficult for optimism to take root in today's offices and factories. The tools of modern management, all too often, facilitate the perception of a natural propensity for failure.

Annual goal setting is but one example. Why do we need to set personal goals for the coming year? Is it because we lack confidence that employees will pursue the right goals left unguided? Or is it because we hope that focus will inspire them to higher levels of performance?

Either justification might be reasonable if the world was static. It is not. The context in which we conduct business is in constant flux, changing in ways and degrees that are difficult to predict.

Like the rest of the universe, no goal exists in isolation. Reality is like a complex ball of twine. Where one influence leaves off and another begins is impossible to know. Like a river, you can never dip your toe in the same reality twice.

Goals, as a result, quickly become outdated, even counterproductive to overcoming the challenges at hand. What to do?

The goals can be changed, of course, but that does not align with the deductive reason for setting goals in the first place. And it is impractical to constantly update goals on the fly. It defeats the purpose. Managers and employees would fill their days doing nothing else.

So what happens?

The employee faces a fork in the road. One option is for the employee to ignore the documented goals and do what is right. "Damn the torpedoes! Full speed ahead," barked US Navy admiral David Glasgow Farragut (1801–1870), at the Battle of Mobile Bay during the American Civil War. To hell with the goals!

This could, of course, be a sign of either great courage and conviction or great naiveté. Come the time for the annual performance review, the cost could be steep.

The more formal and deductive the talent management systems are, the greater the risk. If salary increases are granted on the basis of performance reviews, it would be hard for a manager to justify to the boss or HR manager giving an employee an increase at the top of the range when the employee failed to achieve any goals. Arguing that times have changed will be of great risk to the personal interests of the manager as well. Unless they have a lot of political capital, they are unlikely to assume that risk.

The second option is to pursue the goals despite changing circumstances. This would be a good example of willfully harmful obedience, however, and the result isn't likely to play well at the annual performance review, either. There will no doubt be something said about an apparent unwillingness to embrace change.

The ideal solution, of course, is to sit down and discuss the situation with the boss. That, however, requires a fair amount of trust. Will the boss help to find a solution that will hold up at the year-end review, or will the employee be chastised for a tendency to kick problems upstairs?

When I began my career, I would have, without hesitation, taken the chance and done what I believed to be right under the current circumstances. My advice to young people just beginning their careers today, however, would be to assume nothing. Deduction, I would tell them, eventually takes on a life of its own, and we are long past eventually.

Trust and optimism are intrinsically connected. They are two sides of the same coin of faith. You cannot be optimistic if you don't trust. And you cannot trust if you don't have the faith of optimism.

Ironically, I've come to believe that it is hardship, not success, which builds optimism. I'm really not able to articulate why. Perhaps too much success inevitably makes it seem too easy, although that strikes me as a stronger argument for taking your eye off the ball rather than optimism. Perhaps it is not the hardship, but the recovery that fuels optimism.

At the age of eight, I began to have seizures that sent me crashing to the floor with increasing frequency each day. While I didn't become unconscious, I was not able to speak or control my convulsions during these episodes, as my mother delicately referred to them.

As my seizures were an inevitable distraction in my second-grade public school classroom, I was eventually barred from school and privately tutored at home. I maintained friendships, of course, but I wore protective headgear at all times, and the discomfort naturally created by my seizures among young and old alike inevitably led to a certain degree of personal isolation.

The doctors were baffled. It was 1962, and pediatrics was in its infancy. I ultimately ended up at Boston Children's Hospital, one of the most renowned pediatric institutions in the world, and a teaching hospital affiliated with Harvard Medical School. But even the distinguished team of doctors assigned to my case was ultimately baffled by the origins of the seizures, most concluding that it was a permanent condition.

As I learned from my mother later, however, the lone woman on the team was not ready to accept this conclusion. Rather than discharging me to a life devoid of otherwise normal activities like driving a car, she suggested a pneumoencephalogram, a strictly diagnostic medical procedure that involved removing the fluid from around the brain and replacing it with gas, allowing for a clearer x-ray of the brain. The patient could not be given a general anesthesia, however, due to the need for the brain to operate normally, so the procedure was excruciatingly painful and only used as a last resort, particularly with children. (Thankfully the pneumoencephalogram has been made obsolete by modern scanning technology.)

I can vouch for the discomfort. I still vividly recall lying on the stainless-steel table of what I assume was an operating room, surrounded by a forest of surgical masks and gowns, screaming with all of the conviction I could muster. To the complete surprise of everyone, however, I never had another seizure.

I never learned if the x-rays taken during the procedure helped or not. It didn't matter. The doctors finally concluded that the seizures had been caused by an encephalitic virus or bacteria living in the brain fluid. When the brain fluid was temporarily removed as part of the procedure, it lost its life support and perished.

I never met the woman responsible for my cure after that. I have thought of her often, however, throughout my life. And I have not a whisper of doubt that she is a fundamentally optimistic person who contributed a great deal to the lives of many children.

Perhaps her biggest contribution to my life, however, was not the elimination of my seizures. They were not life threatening, and I am sure I could have still led a fulfilling life, as many others in similar circumstances have. I couldn't have played Little League Baseball or Pop Warner Football, but I'm sure my meager athletic talents would not have been missed.

She gave me the greatest gift of all, the gift that I believe was behind whatever success I have known in my life. She gave me the conviction of optimism. She taught me that the logic of deduction isn't the only way to look at problems. Sometimes you just have to believe.

As discussed in chapter 10, I believe that it is obligation that leads to trust in a relationship. If your partner, boss, employee, or colleague, believes in the sincerity of your obligation to them, they will trust you. It is an autonomic reflex.

Some obligation is earned. If someone saves your life, it is only natural to feel some sense of obligation. More often than not, however, obligation requires a leap of faith of its own. You must believe in the virtue of obligation itself.

That obligation can be hard to come by in today's business climate. The owners of our largest corporations are institutional investors who feel little sense of obligation toward the employees of the companies they invest in. The deductive tools of business and talent management likewise impede obligation in the name of objectivity and a self-imposed commitment to making the tough decisions.

Only optimism nurtures obligation. Only optimism fosters the trust that is so critical to individual fulfillment and organizational performance.

Twenty-Two

Enabling Rationalization

My first major in college was mathematics. I later switched to economics but flirted with the idea of becoming an econometrician, an economist who works with statistical models. And after graduation I took a job as a financial analyst in the corporate finance department of a multinational US company. As a result, I'm fairly comfortable moving around a P&L, a balance sheet, and a financial model.

In theory, almost any business decision can be financially modeled. All business decisions have some financial implication. When I interviewed for the aforementioned job, the CFO said to me, "The beauty of this job is that every decision made in this company has a financial implication. So we can stick our nose in everyone else's business."

He's right, of course. The legal department makes a similar argument, as does HR and investor relations, communications, and the like. There is never a shortage of cooks in the kitchen at most companies.

There are, however, a couple of big risks in treating every business decision as a financial one. One is that financial models naturally rely on historical data. There is no such thing as a future fact. There is only speculation and hypothesis. Modelers can incorporate future assumptions to try and give the model some forward-looking sensitivity. In the end, however, it's all speculation. Informed speculation, perhaps, but speculation nonetheless. No one knows with certainty what the future will bring.

The other Achilles' heel of financial models is the fact that some variables may not be measurable. The modeler must ignore them or rely on proxy data that may have to be subjectively modified to make it usable. Hopefully, nothing is lost in the translation, but it often is.

In the end, financial models are easily manipulated. Not always consciously, of course. But the modeler will be unable to fully disentangle his or her own biases. The modeler is the artist and may have great freedom to handpick the variables and data to build into the model. If ten years of data doesn't make the case expected, perhaps five years will. Or three.

If you are requesting approval for a big project or capital investment, the request will probably be assigned to a financial analyst for validation. The finance folks are smart. They know that the model you submitted with the request for authorization undoubtedly looked at the investment in the best possible light.

If that happens, ask the modeler what variables will be built into his or her model. That will tell you volumes about whether or not the modeler intuitively supports the idea or not. If so, it will probably survive the scrutiny. If not, assume the worst. The truly open mind is rare and ha-ha moments seldom emerge when crunching the numbers.

I have a longtime friend who once served as the CAO of a public company that owned its own aircraft. The CEO loved planes but was genuinely cognizant of his fiduciary responsibilities to the shareholders. Every year, therefore, he instructed the CAO to construct a financial model to determine whether or not the plane could be objectively justified.

And every year it passed the test. The CEO had a financial model in the files that supported his decision to keep the plane, and the CAO did what he was asked to do. Did he fudge the analysis? Not at all. His model was entirely defensible—if, that is, you were willing to accept that owning a private aircraft *could* be justified. If you weren't so inclined, the model probably didn't matter anyway.

I honestly think the CAO was doing the right thing. One of his jobs was to keep the CEO focused on the financial issues that were most critical to the long-term health of the company. The plane, no doubt, wasn't one of them. The more time he spent modeling the plane in an attempt to convince the CEO to sell it, the less time they would both have to focus on things that mattered more.

The corporate power structure has changed considerably over the last few decades. In the past, the CFO, except in financial services company, was seldom the number two voice in the corporate structure. That role normally fell to someone in one of the functional areas like marketing, sales, or operations, depending on the company, the people involved, and the industry.

Today, however, the CFO is often the second most powerful individual in the corporate hierarchy. And, as always, there are a multitude of reasons for that shift. Shareholder activism, increased financial risk, the sheer amount of face time the CEO and CFO typically spend with each other, and the fact that many CEOs themselves came up through the financial ranks, all play a part.

Recent case law, moreover, has clearly established the potential personal liability of directors and senior managers when corporate decisions go bad. As a result, when management presents a new idea or proposal to the board, the first question typically asked is, "Has this been modeled?"

Microsoft and its Excel spreadsheet application, of course, have only accelerated the trend of increased modeling. Creating a financial model has never been easier. My young daughter, not yet in high school, already knows how. And link the model with some of the easy to use charting software available and almost anyone can create a professional-looking presentation that screams credibility, even if the seemingly obvious solution that appears to jump out of the model is, in fact, in error.

For all of these reasons, financial models are now the currency of corporate decision making. Many line and unit managers often spend more time updating their financial models, often to satisfy someone higher up in the hierarchy, than they spend actually creating value for the customer. (And profits for the shareholder.)

Models are not bad per se. Intellectually, they are rationally appealing. And they can be of immense value. They can, however, be a deceitful tool for false rationalization.

There is an old saying that, "Figures don't lie, but liars figure." No one seems to know for sure who said it first (it is often attributed to Mark Twain), but it has been around for a long time, and, like most venerable nuggets of wisdom, there is a lot of truth to the observation.

To paraphrase a sentiment offered in chapter 9, computers have greatly enhanced the arsenal of the liar, although when it comes to numbers and statistics, the modeler may not be conscious of the deception. Artisans often put form before function, wittingly or not.

In the March 2011 issue of *Harvard Business Review*, writers Christensen, Alton, Rising, and Waldeck note that companies spend more than $2 trillion on acquisitions per year and 70 percent to 90 percent of them fail. How can that possibly be?

Those acquisitions were all supported by financial models built by some of the brightest financial minds in the universe. Investment bankers do this for a living. Surely, they know what questions to ask and can smell a faulty model from the next county.

And they can. But just as employers often make the unconscious decision to hire a candidate in the first sixty seconds of the job interview, most CEOs have decided just how badly they want to make an acquisition long before the investment bankers boot up their laptops and start to build the model to support the idea. And the people who feed the bankers the information they need to build the model probably know just how bad the CEO wants this deal to happen. And, of course, they are only human, and the CEO is the boss.

The worst that can happen is that the negotiations drag on. The players become increasingly invested in a successful outcome. Somewhere down the line, "deal lust" sets in, and any remaining objectivity is jettisoned overboard in order to keep the deal afloat. The input to the model gets modified, and, voila, it's a go! The model says this acquisition makes sense.

The best investment bankers understand this truth all too well. If you take part in such a negotiation, you will note that the investment bankers don't so much sell the deal as they try to convince the other side that they, the other side, really want this to happen. You can almost see them ever so gently scattering the pixie dust of lust around the table.

This is nothing new, of course. Many of the most significant M&A deals of years past were rumored to be made on the golf course or in the overstuffed leather chairs of an urban private club, brandies in hand. I knew a CEO, in fact, who openly admitted that he successfully negotiated his biggest acquisition on the eleventh hole. There was a handshake long before the bankers were even contacted.

The root underlying problem is that inductive logic has been completely discredited in the halls of corporate America. It has acquired the reputation of a soft science, like psychology or sociology. While there is such a thing as an inductive mathematical proof, mathematical induction is an inference rule from which inductive reason is excluded. Confusing, huh?

Is reality objectively and deductively definable? That is the real question. All scientists and many executives say "yes." It is a seductive conclusion. But, I believe, it is a false conclusion. I have witnessed and experienced countless events in my life that are not readily explained using the tools of deduction. And while some of them may ultimately be explained by future scientific discovery, I have every confidence that some will remain a mystery.

The scientific discovery that will ultimately put it all in perspective, I trust, will be the realization that deductive and inductive logic are not so far apart. One will be as sound as the other once we understand what really gives substance to reality.

Here's how I define the distinction between deduction and induction. My explanation relies on a painting by George Seurat, entitled *Sunday Afternoon on the Island of La Grande Jatte*. I'm sure you've seen it. It is a very pleasant painting of a crowd of French gentlemen and ladies strolling about a park, all gussied up, parasols in hand, in the late nineteenth century. It was painted in the pointillist tradition, which Seurat founded using tiny dots of pigment rather than brush strokes.

Think of the dots as observable facts. The image is truth. And when the dots are all in place, the truth is easy to deduce. The image is obvious and cannot be mistaken for anything other than what it is.

What if 10 percent of the dots were removed, however? Fifty percent? Ninety percent? At some point (excuse the pun), the viewer is left to conjecture what the image represents. It is at that point that the viewer is forced to rely on induction rather than deduction.

The overall image, however, has not changed. We just can't see it all and either have to ask the artist, who may or may not be available, or induce possible truths.

The *Merriam-Webster* online dictionary defines the origin and etymology of the word "true" as follows:

> Middle English *trewe*, from Old English *trēowe* faithful; akin to Old High German gi*triuwi* faithful, Old Irish *derb* sure, and probably to Sanskrit *dāruṇa* hard, *dāru* wood
>
> (Retrieved May 1, 2017, from merriam-webster.com at https://www.merriam-webster.com/dictionary/true[1])

In ancient times, in other words, truth and faith were essentially the same thing. Only in modern times have they come to represent very different things indeed. And the same is true, to a large extent, with deduction and induction.

In the same way that modern science has squeezed faith out of truth, the science of management has sought to squeeze induction out of sound reasoning. Both developments are a product of false rationalization.

It is impossible to avoid induction in the everyday world of life and commerce. David Hume, an eighteenth century philosopher and author of *Treatise of Human Nature*, was the first to fully recognize this. He noted that we routinely eat bread because we induce from experience that it is safe and will keep us healthy. It's entirely possible, however, that our next loaf could kill us. Were we to demand deductively substantiated proof of its safety before eating any and all food, we would literally die of starvation.

Rationalization, in other words, is often just an attempt to recast faith by using the language of deduction. Even when the rationalization is deductively sound, however, it may not be complete. There may be other factors, as yet undiscovered or deceptively undisclosed, that play an important role.

This is exactly why Sir Karl Raimund Popper (1902–1994), one of the greatest philosophers of science of the twentieth century noted, "Our knowledge can only be finite, while our ignorance must necessarily be infinite." Or, as Albert Einstein put it, "Whoever undertakes to set himself up as a judge of truth and knowledge is shipwrecked by the laughter of the gods."

As a result, the most important weapon in the arsenal of logic with which we battle in the world of business is not deduction or induction; it is doubt. The most rational of proposals and ideas can never be assumed to be valid. It can only be valid as far as the argument goes. But what lies beyond? We can't know what we don't know.

The further that business has moved along the continuum of deduction, the more we have come to demonize doubt and ennoble rationality. Clearly, however, we have fallen deeply into the trap of false fallacy. The choice is not either/or. At best it is a choice of degrees.

My advice is that when in doubt, doubt more. Doubt is not a roadblock. It is a catalyst for discovery. There is an old Zen saying that I think says it best: "Great Doubt: great awakening. Little Doubt: little awakening. No Doubt: no awakening."

Doubt keeps our exploration alive. It prevents us from cutting our exploration short prematurely, from reaching conclusions while there is more evidence to be discovered. Doubt keeps our eyes forward. It is the motivation to raise one foot from the terra firma of existing knowledge in anticipation of placing it down again on new, as yet undiscovered, terrain.

Beware, as well, of the rational argument. Just as we can't exist without induction, rationality is not the supreme arbiter of truth. Never be afraid of what you can't articulate. The lack of explanation makes the truth no less true.

Twenty-Three

Work-Life Balance

When I began my career, you didn't hear much talk about work-life balance. Work was work, and achievement in your work was life. Balance was all about getting ahead.

For a long time that was enough for me. By the early '90s, I had achieved much, as I then measured achievement. I was the president of a well-known multinational company, I had a corner office, and I had the wealth to support a very comfortable lifestyle. I went skiing in the Rockies one week and sailing in the Caribbean the next.

But I could hardly get out of bed in the morning. What was the point? Like so many others before and after me, I began to realize that all that I had achieved did not bring the fulfillment I expected. The victory was hollow.

I chased all of the usual remedies. I worked harder. I pushed myself in exercise to a point well beyond healthy exertion. (I would later learn that my appearance led many friends and colleagues to assume that I was privately fighting serious illness.) In short, I tried to escape in every way imaginable.

The children, of course, were watching me and my generational compatriots crash on the rocks of blind ambition. And they have vowed not to make the same mistakes, just as every generation has vowed not to repeat the worst excesses and failings of their parents.

To be fair, not all of the tectonic shift in values that has put a greater premium on work-life balance has been stimulated by internalized choice. As the American workplace has become increasingly dehumanized, largely through an excessive preoccupation with the tools and protocols of deduction, the American worker, young and old alike, has been forced to seek personal fulfillment elsewhere.

If the American workplace has achieved greater efficiency and strength, and I see little evidence of that, it has come at a price in human disenchantment. Corporate credibility, loyalty, and pride have all been compromised.

Charles Wilson (1890–1961), the CEO of General Motors also known as "Engine Charlie" to differentiate him from another Charles Wilson, the CEO of GE, known as "Electric Charlie," was the secretary of defense under President Dwight D. Eisenhower from 1953 to 1957. During his confirmation hearing, Engine Charlie is rumored to have said, "What is good for GM is good for the country." (There is evidence that what he really said is that what is good for the country is good for GM.)

Whatever Mr. Wilson actually said, the sentiment as rumored probably didn't raise many eyebrows at the time. I suspect most Americans shared the perspective. Corporate America has lost much of its prestige in the court of public opinion since then, however. It is now public enemy number one or two, depending on where you slot the politicians, as well personified by the vitriol spewed at United Airlines through social media following an incident in April 2017 in which a passenger was dragged off an overbooked United Airlines flight so that one of the company's employees could have his seat.

"It's not personal, it's business," has been a common villainous phrase in the movies for a long time. Seldom, however, has the sentiment risen to the level of indignation that it evokes today. Whether valid or not on a business-by-business basis, it is an increasingly common sentiment toward large American corporations.

Business leaders do get it. They understand that to the extent they dehumanize the business in the eyes of customers and employees, they sow the seeds of distrust and disillusionment. And they have, to varying degrees, attempted to get the humanity back.

United Airlines, ironically, defines its "Shared Purpose" as "Uniting people. Connecting the World." Wells Fargo, which has admitted to massive fraud in its sales practices, publicly touts its "culture of caring."

The message, however, is not getting through. And it is the lack of perceived sincerity that is to blame. Sincerity is another facet of trust that calibrates the perception against the reality. If a message is not perceived as sincere, it does more than undermine its own credibility; it taints and demonizes the messenger.

The path of sincerity is built on a footing of consistency. If an individual's or company's behavior is not consistent, doubt will shroud every message. Intent will never be realized.

Consistency is particularly important in the workplace. When employees have come to me for adjudication of perceived injustices over the years, I have always been careful to point out that my obligation as a leader was not just to ensure that the punishment fit the crime in this case but that I could reach the same conclusion when the next person walked through my door under the same circumstances.

If employees perceive that some people receive preferential treatment—that you play favorites—you simply cannot lead. You have surrendered the mantle of governance.

Robert Fulghum, the best-selling author, said it best in the very title of his celebrated book, *All I Really Need to Know I Learned in Kindergarten*. It's true. You have to walk the talk, an admonition that's uttered up and down the halls of corporate America on a daily basis. So why don't we live by it?

The simple reason is that we have abandoned what we learned in kindergarten. Specifically, we have abandoned induction, faith, and doubt. We have forgotten that conjecture is the fuel of dreams. We have forgotten that faith is the language of the possible. We have forgotten that doubt is the analytical path to eventual enlightenment.

Everyone wants a life that is fulfilling and satisfying. We all want to work in a way and in an environment that is stimulating and rewarding. Nobody really wants to report to a daily grind. Nobody wants to spend as much time as most of us do working in a place that is not comforting and secure.

Americans spend approximately one-third of their lives at work. If that time is spent in an environment that we consider hostile to our happiness and connection with the people around us, we will carve it out of our lives either figuratively or literally. We will compartmentalize our work and that, in turn, will inevitably lead to a decline in our performance. Angst begets failure. Stress hones disillusionment and the loss of commitment.

I began this chapter by discussing the fact that early in my career I pursued the false god of achievement and material success and how that led to an inevitable disillusionment and lack of personal fulfillment. But that was only part of the story.

All stories exist in context, and mine is no exception. In this case the context is the culture of workplace in which we toil and the culture in which we live. As the logic of deduction has come to increasingly dominate the way in which we live and conduct business, we have inadvertently promoted the human propensity to embrace ideology and the institutions built upon it. This, in turn, has opened the door to the emergence and domination of the me-centric *-isms* (e.g., individualism, consumerism, hedonism, egoism) that have come to define the dark side of modern society and the modern workplace.

We have likewise created, or at least exaggerated, the life/work dilemma by making it a false dilemma fallacy. By dehumanizing the workplace, we have forced compartmentalization and the choice it requires. Employees must now make a choice between life and work that wasn't previously necessary.

I am not a nostalgic person, and I don't want to throw up the proverbial slow pitch for skeptics to hit out of the park. Whatever my motivations for saying so, the truth is still the truth. We have dehumanized the workplace, and we have done it to ourselves through our zealous development of the science of management as defined through the singular logic of deduction.

We have merely to readopt the traditional definition of truth discussed previously, to give the soft values of induction (i.e., trust, hope, inclusion) the same weight that we give to the hard values of deduction (i.e., accountability, winning, objectification) in the way we manage the workplace and conduct our commerce.

Twenty-Four

Labels

Think about the people you work with. What comes to mind as you consider each one? My guess is that you've got a label for most of them. I do the same thing.

Why do we do that? As with precognitive conclusion, the simple answer is efficiency. Our brain can't keep up with the demands placed upon it to reach conclusions, so we resort to shorthand. And shorthand, like all language, is imprecise. It is not all encompassing. It's largely limited to two or three dimensions in a four- or five-dimension world.

Deduction enhances the proclivity. Scientists love to label things. If a scientist uncovers a new truth about the universe or the physical world, there is an inevitable desire to label it as the law of such and such, or the so and so phenomenon.

Doctors and medical researchers do the same thing. Even the most obscure diseases and conditions are given names. Labels mark the path of medical progress and the discovery of knowledge.

Business is not immune to the temptation. If a company launches a new project or initiative, someone is sure to want to label it. Processes are routinely labeled. Departments put labels on the entry door. Files are labeled, as are pipes and network cables.

Labels can be very helpful. They help us to stay organized and can save time and money when IT needs to move a terminal or someone in maintenance wants to know what the blue valve controls.

Companies increasingly like to label their employees as well. They document their personality type and their social styles. In addition to documenting their hard skills like degrees and certifications earned, they document their soft skills like the ability to communicate or their ability to solve complex problems.

In theory, of course, labeling helps to inventory an organization's skills and identify skill gaps. It also assists in hiring and personnel assignment. Who can argue the benefits of aligning skills and experience to make sure the right people are in the right jobs?

In practice, however, attempting to label the organization carries the same risks as financial modeling. It assumes you can assess a person's skills both objectively and in total. What if, however, an employee has never been put in a situation where critical skills have been put to the test and thus remain largely hidden from view?

Veterans will tell you that it is impossible to predict exactly how a soldier will react in actual combat. Do we know ourselves how we will react to traumatic events in our lives?

Skills and abilities are like the data used in a financial model. They are limited to past observation. Yet the one thing that we can assume with confidence is that the future will not look like the past. Change is inevitable. Can we, with any degree of confidence, map previously demonstrated skills against future events?

Probably not. Organizations and the jobs that define them don't exist in isolation. They are part of a dynamic ecosystem defined by a multitude of external influences and self-imposed changes.

In the end, attempts to map an individual's or an organization's skills are not unlike the attempts by professional sports teams to model player potential through extensive testing of basic athletic and mental skills. And both have met with similar results.

Results from the NFL combine, as discussed in an earlier chapter, have shown little correlation to actual player performance in the NFL. Tom Brady, the quarterback for the New England Patriots, is one of only two NFL players in history to win five Super Bowls and is considered by many to be one of the best quarterbacks in NFL history. He was, however, drafted in the sixth round of the 2000 draft and ranks sixty-fourth in speed among NFL quarterbacks according to an October 3, 2016, ranking on bleacherreport.com.

The risks to a business of excessive labeling, moreover, go beyond mere ineffectiveness. The process of deductive analysis often becomes a ruse for other forms of organizational engineering, such as the political homogenization of the organization and the elimination of all forms of diversity in thought and world view.

Here is a Philosophy 101 question for you: If a liar admits to lying, are they telling the truth? How do you know the admission is not a lie?

You don't, of course. The answer is in the eye of the beholder. You can only speculate.

In the 1990 movie, *My Blue Heaven*, Steve Martin stars as a snitch on the organized crime family he was part of. When the government finally puts him on the stand and he is cross-examined, the defense lawyer for the crime bosses begins challenging his credibility by asking questions about what the government was doing for him in exchange for his testimony. After a few such questions, Martin's character says something along the lines of, "Look, if you're suggesting that I'm saying all of this because of what the Feds are doing for me, you've got a good point." Then he pauses and says, leaning forward in the witness box, "But the truth is still the truth."

And therein lies the problem with attempts to individual skills and behavior. They may be accurate part of the time. But are they accurate all of the time? And how will you determine which time this is?

If an employee has been labeled as disruptive, does that mean they appeared to behave disruptively on one or two occasions or that they behave disruptively every day of the week? What it does mean, if the assessment ends up on paper, is that the supervisor has a permanent reason for taking punitive action for almost any reason since they now have the cover of a documented label. And it happens every day of the week.

In the end, however, labels aren't the real problem. The real risk of labels is the deductive way in which the label is interpreted and applied.

In the eyes of the Chinese, if you were not born to Chinese parents, you are a foreigner and the Chinese will openly refer to you in that way. If you speak fluent Mandarin, you are merely a foreigner who speaks Chinese. If you have lived in China all of your life, you are merely a foreigner who grew up in China. Even if you have a Chinese wife, as I do, you are a foreigner with a Chinese wife.

When I lived in China I was commonly referred to as a foreigner. I was likewise frequently told that I had very round eyes, very white skin, and a big nose. Babies often grabbed my nose, and when I got off the beaten path of urban China, staring was the norm.

At first, of course, it was all a bit uncomfortable, to be honest. Until, that is, I realized how deductively biased my Western sensibilities were. Once I came to understand the inductive foundation of Chinese culture and was able to put the words and behaviors in that context (there's that word again), the pejorative perception disappeared. I had been projecting intent through the lens of my own biased logic.

The problem with attempting to label people in an organizational setting, in other words, is not the attempt per se, but the way in which such attempts are ultimately used. In the excessively deductive world view of modern business, everything is either cause or effect. Everything is either/or. You are either moving ahead or moving backward. There is no neutral.

As a result, words have meaning. And sometimes the meaning that is ascribed to them isn't the meaning originally intended.

The end result is that the attempt to deductively manage people has, on average, been no more successful than attempts to deductively manage acquisitions or capital projects. There is an appearance of objectivity that just doesn't hold up under scrutiny.

As noted earlier in the book, if you have ever ridden in a car in China, you know that chaos and anarchy reign supreme. To the uninitiated it is a harrowing experience to say the least.

In fact, the rules of the road in China are very much in line with the rules in place everywhere else. The difference is that the rules aren't enforced. And because the Chinese are inherently inductive, they feel no sense of obligation to abide by them voluntarily.

If our factory drivers came upon a freeway on-ramp that was backed up with traffic, they just went up the exit ramp and cut in. Every square inch of pavement was put to use in heavy traffic and traffic lanes ceased to exist. Speed limits carry no meaning, and driving the wrong way on a one-way street or divided highway is perfectly acceptable, even to the police, if it gets you to where you want to go faster.

I traveled ninety kilometers to work every day and consequently spent a lot of time in the car. And yet, in my entire nine years in China, I never once witnessed a single case of road rage. I never once saw a middle finger or fist raised in protest. Never. I frequently thought, however, that if a similar incident had occurred in the United States, there would surely be guns drawn and fists flying. Middle fingers and cursing at the least.

In inductive cultures, "Sometimes a cigar is just a cigar," as Freud famously observed. In the increasingly deductive atmosphere of Western culture, however, a cigar is almost always something else. Being a cigar is just too inductive. It's too devoid of symbolism and meaning for the excessively deductive mind.

Deduction is the siren's song of a reliable and knowable reality. It is the language of the learned and the rational, devoid of superstition and chance.

Or so we tell ourselves. Falsely so.

Twenty-Five

My Inductive Mother

My mother was an extraordinary woman. Unfortunately I didn't always appreciate the full extent of that truth. Nor did I fully comprehend what made her exceptional.

Both of my parents were part of the greatest generation and served in the military during World War II. My father joined the navy out of high school and was assigned to a destroyer escort in the European theater. My mother was a registered nurse in the Nurses Corps, an adjunct of the US Navy. Like many of their generation, neither parent ever talked about the experience. That's essentially the limit of my knowledge.

It didn't take a lot of insight, however, to know that my mother had dealt with great human tragedy and suffering. She served most of the war in a stateside military hospital where those with the most serious battle injuries were sent.

It is easy to appreciate, as a result, why she pursued a career in pediatric nursing after the war. She undoubtedly needed to regain some sense of emotional balance.

While she was emotionally strong, and could be tough indeed were the welfare of her children threatened, I have yet to meet a less judgmental person in my life. She literally never had a bad word to say about anyone.

She also embraced the legend of Santa Claus for the entirety of her eight decades of life. I always dismissed this belief, unfortunately, as simple playfulness, or a yearning for the innocence of youth. To be honest, I was judgmental. I never said it out loud, but she knew. It just made her smile. She knew I would eventually come around.

I now realize I had it all wrong. She was plenty smart and experienced enough to know that Santa was a legend. It was, however, a legend she embraced. Perhaps not true in the worldliest sense, but true at some other level of life and consciousness. Most beliefs, in the end, come down to a question of personal choice, and she chose to believe in Santa. She liked the idea and what it stood for.

It was the Chinese who ultimately taught me the why behind the what of my mother's extraordinary nature. It came as an epiphany as I sought to understand the cultural differences between the deductive and the inductive world view. My mother had an inductive world view. She would have fit right in in China.

More accurately, she had found a pleasing equilibrium between the deductive and the inductive. She was a nurse, after all. She had a firm commitment to the scientific method and the concept of cause and effect. She believed in modern medicine with all her heart. She complemented that philosophy, however, with an acceptance of that which she couldn't explain.

She often noted, for example, that the night shift in the ER and on the maternity ward was the busiest when there was a full moon. All the nurses in the large Boston hospital where she worked after the war, she claimed, tracked the moon's phases on their duty calendars so that they knew when to expect a heavy workload. And she never expressed a personal need to understand why. The cause and effect didn't matter. It just was.

And I believe it was her experience during the war that pushed her in that inductive direction. Having given the matter a lot of thought since, in fact, I have come to believe that severe life trauma often pushes people to the left on the inductive-deductive continuum. They become both more tolerant and more accepting of things they can't fully explain.

That, in turn, makes them better people. Just like my mother.

Twenty-Six

The Hiring Process

In 1993 I was recognized by the World Economic Forum (WEF) of Davos, Switzerland fame, as one of two hundred individuals from around the world to make up its inaugural class of Global Leaders for Tomorrow (GFT). The program was designed to identify two hundred individuals, all born after 1950 (which at that time was a lot younger) that had both already achieved recognized success in their chosen field of endeavor and were likely to shape social, economic, and political events in the future.

The objective was not to recognize us individually per se but to provide a forum for us to network, get to know each other, and collaborate for the benefit of future generations. It was heady stuff. When I went to a luncheon of GFTs hosted by Klaus Schwab himself, held at the Grand Hyatt in Hong Kong, each attendee was asked to stand and introduce him- or herself. As I recall, I was sitting between the treasury secretary of Mexico and a prince of one of the Scandinavian countries.

When my turn arrived, I rose slowly and looked around the room with some trepidation. I finally said, "In introducing myself I must first and foremost admit that I am most surely here by mistake." It was a deadpan delivery because I was deadpan serious and, of course, I got a polite chuckle out of the room.

What that and several other experiences have taught me beyond the shadow of a doubt, however, is that all people are cut from the same cloth. Or, as my father used to say, "We all put on our britches the same way, one leg at a time." It is true.

We are, however, all different. And we all differ in different ways. Each is unique, and the path we follow in life is truly impossible to predict ahead of time. Don't bother trying is my advice.

How, then, do we know who to recruit to the team? While the current achievement of the nominees could be interpreted with some objectivity, how did the WEF know with any precision who would ultimately influence the world and who would escape to a secluded beach somewhere? (Looking back on the list now, they picked a few of both.)

As part of the WEF selection process, I was interviewed by a prestigious executive search firm in Fort Worth, Texas. At the end of the interview, I asked the senior partner participating in the interview if he might offer his take on the résumé I had been requested to prepare. While I wasn't consciously looking to leave my current job, I wanted to get his perception of my background from the perspective of a potential corporate employer. It had been a while since I had been in the market, and I wanted to be prepared.

He scanned my résumé one more time to gather his thoughts and said, "The one thing that will jump out for a potential employer is that you've been at one company for a long period of time."

"That used to be called loyalty," I noted, with a self-conscious chuckle.

"Fair enough, and you've had no reason to leave. You've consistently moved up the organization, and your list of accomplishments is impressive. The game has changed, however, and potential employers are inclined to conclude (deductively, of course) that a person who stays with a company for a long period of time is either not particularly strong or not particularly motivated."

Approximately one decade later, I was interested in teaching at the college level. I had always had a passion for learning and thought that sharing that passion with others, served up on a lifetime of experience and no small measure of success, would allow me to contribute in a way that I found personally fulfilling. It was not, however, to be.

I was not applying to Harvard or Princeton, mind you. I liked where I was living and my financial needs were relatively modest, so I applied to small local universities and community colleges. Some were actually quite obscure and, I thought, should be pleased to have me on the team.

But it was not to be. I not only wasn't hired, but I never even got an interview. And I couldn't imagine why, until some sympathetic soul finally spilled the beans. "You have no advanced degree. Without that no college will even look at you. It really doesn't matter what other skills or experience you bring to the position, the institution cannot risk having a name on its letterhead without an educational suffix. It would dilute the brand."

That I understood.

So I redirected my effort and decided to try my hand at writing. Actually, I had written my entire life, although never for publication. I do enjoy the written word and believe that writing forces clarity of thought, particularly in the days prior to the laptop computer. As a person who has always liked to think, writing has always been a tool for honing that skill.

I worked hard, bought all the books on how the publishing game is played, and eventually found a succession of agents willing to try their hand with my writing career. They were all, as was I, ultimately disappointed. Although I have to admit that their disappointment typically arrived after one or two failed attempts to sell the book to a publisher. I was a little more resilient.

And, once again, a sympathetic soul ultimately set me straight. "James Joyce probably wouldn't get published today. Publishing now is all about getting the most out of the authors who have already established a brand. Long shots just aren't worth the risk anymore."

I did ultimately go on to be published, but the experiences described above have never been forgotten. The lesson learned, however, may not be the one that initially comes to mind.

The tools we use to evaluate a person's potential—the tools we use to decide who to hire—have changed rather dramatically over the years. We can't ask someone their age or their marital status, but we can profile social styles and temperament through standardized testing. We can scour the applicant's social media footprint for personal insight that potential employers were heretofore reliant on the applicant's honesty to be aware of. And while the risk of liability has killed the traditional reference, Google has made everyone's life a matter of public record. Despite all of the new regulations relating to privacy in the United States, we have never known more about the personal life of each other.

Never before, in other words, have we had more access to more information about the candidates we consider. Never before has there been more transparency. Never before have we been able to defend our choices with more seemingly deductive facts and arguments.

But has it led to better hiring decisions? There is no empirical or anecdotal evidence to suggest it has. In fact, I would argue, just the opposite is true. While deduction can be illuminating, it can also be a place to hide. While we still evaluate prospects on inductive criteria, we can now more easily make selections on the wrong criteria and justify the decision on the deceptive foundation of deduction.

Do we hire the candidate who shows the most potential, or the candidate that has the least risk to make us look bad should the decision prove to be a mistake? Does the candidate have the skills we need to defeat our competitive foes, or are we attracted by skills that would be useful in defeating our internal political foes? Are we attracted to the candidate that adds to our diversity, or the candidate that will merely fit in?

Subjective judgments, of course, can be just as dangerous and misleading as honest attempts at objective evaluation that are nonetheless misguided. Walt Disney, legend has it, insisted that candidates for speaking roles in his animated films sit behind a screen when they auditioned. He didn't want physical appearance to cloud his judgment.

But just as liars can be telling the truth, inductive judgments aren't always subjective, and when they are, they aren't always wrong.

Intuition and instinct, as I argued in chapter 14, can be powerful sources of truth. We can't entirely explain why, but that alone doesn't disprove the potential.

In the end, therefore, I believe there are two qualities, above all else, that you should look for in potential hires—humility and integrity. No leader who has survived the test of time has ever succeeded without both. And while you may not think you need to hire a leader to fill a specific job vacancy, you can never have too many leaders because all successful people must be leaders at some level. Even the soloists among us are part of a large team in one way or another.

The benefits of humility and integrity, I believe, are self-evident. Humility is essential to the ability to learn and grow. And, of course, humble people are just more enjoyable to be around. And while that may sound self-serving, there is nothing to say that self-serving truths are invalid in some broader sense.

Integrity, of course, is all about trust and doing the right thing. But it goes beyond that. Integrity is the scale by which courage and self-confidence are appropriately measured. The appearance of self-confidence is just that. True self-confidence, an essential ingredient to achieving one's potential, is marked by the willingness to accept notions of right and wrong bigger than our self-interest.

Beyond humility and integrity, you want diversity. You want people who think differently than you do and who add another dimension, for whatever reason, to the team's skill set and shared world view.

I was the CEO of a company located in a manufacturing neighborhood on the outskirts of Detroit. There was no shortage of diners in the area catering to an industrial clientele that I found to be an excellent place to conduct the final step in a promising job interview. It wasn't fast food, but you could get a decent meal for two for $10. The chair and table might wobble, but the servers were generally salt of the earth—good, hardworking people.

The reason for taking the promising applicants to lunch there was not to instill frugality in someone who might be spending money from the same till. It was to see how they treated the help. If they were arrogant, dismissive, or condescending in any way, an offer would not be forthcoming. Even silence wasn't enough. I wanted only executives who acknowledged those who served them with a pleasant and sincere please and thank you. No exceptions.

Perhaps my best advice on this front, however, is not to overthink the process. Don't be afraid to go with your instinct. It will often save a lot of time and money. I think it's okay not to hire a candidate that you are inclined to hire if you didn't feel that way in the first ten minutes. At the very least, it's cause for revalidating the decision.

Above all else, look beyond the hard facts listed on the CV and the results of the standardized testing. Look at the person.

Above all else, make your decision with the confidence—and fear—that for whatever reason you hire someone, what really matters is what you do for them the day they show up for work.

Twenty-Seven

What's the Attraction?

Why is deduction so alluring to the Western mind? The short answer is that we are a curious people with a predilection toward science that is always searching for objective cause and effect. But which is cause? And which is effect? And which comes first?

An understanding of cause and effect, of course, is the first step toward gaining some sense of control over events. And as discussed previously, it is a sense of control that alleviates stress. To the extent that we can understand the forces behind the events, we have some chance to control the events. And to avoid the debilitating stress that results when we feel we are simply bobbing along like a leaf on a swift current.

But every emotion exists in context, and stress is no exception. And context, I believe, is a circular universe. It is not linear as we are often tempted to believe.

In the case of stress, a sense of control can alleviate stress. To a point. What if we truly believed that we are in complete control of the world and the people around us? Would we feel less stress?

No, because stress is multidimensional and circular. Control alleviates stress up to a point. If we have total control, however, and bad things continue to happen—and they will—we will then suffer the stress of believing that we could have controlled something but did not.

To believe that bad things will happen anyway, of course, requires an inductive leap of faith. I feel that is quite a deductive conclusion to make, however, based on the empirical data available. Have you ever known anyone who never had to confront sadness or loss? Doesn't the very finite duration of life itself guarantee that loss ultimately finds all of us?

Particularly religious and spiritual people, of course, appear to be more at peace with death than those who do not share their faith. But why is that? Is it not because they are viewing death and loss through the lens of an inductive leap of faith?

Some believe that science is the religion of "real" logic and fact. Science, however, as I have now noted repeatedly, is not a body of knowledge or beliefs in the way that an organized religion is. Science is a methodology for interpreting reality. And it is fallible.

Sam Harris (b. 1967) is one of the world's most famous and influential atheists. In addition to writing several books, Harris cofounded Project Reason, which now appears to be defunct. Its website, however, initially stated that the purpose of the project was to "encourage critical thinking and erode the influence of dogmatism, superstition, and bigotry in our world." (Quotation taken from an article on thebestschools.org website, a leading resource for campus and online education: http://www.thebestschools.org/blog/2011/12/01/50-top-atheists-in-the-world-today/.)

But if a liar can tell the truth why does superstition have to be false?

Here's the first definition of superstition offered by the *Merriam-Webster* online dictionary:

1a: a belief or practice resulting from ignorance, fear of the unknown, trust in magic or chance, or a false conception of causation **b:** an irrational abject attitude of mind toward the supernatural, nature, or God resulting from superstition

(Retrieved April 18, 2017, from merriam-webster.com at https://www.merriam-webster.com/dictionary/superstition)

By that definition, I suppose, superstition is inherently bad. But is superstition always "a false conception of causation"? That just doesn't sound right. And I'm not even sure it can be classified as scientific since there is plenty of empirical evidence that it is not universally true. It may not itself be universally true, and the perceived causation may be coincidental rather than causal, but if no other explanation can be provided, why does it follow, even deductively, that it must be wrong?

To believe that superstition and chance are always in error requires its own leap of faith. While acknowledging the potential for superstition and chance to be causally true may be "irrational," it is only deductively so.

Said differently, if deductive logic is taken to its logical extreme, does it not become inductive? And does not the person who lives by superstition and the power of magic alone ultimately forge a logical context of deductive beliefs and behaviors?

It was Canadian scholar, Marshall McLuhan (1911–1980), who said, "The medium is the message." Contrary to popular misconception, McLuhan was not talking about the media as we think of it today. He defined a medium as an extension of ourselves. The table saw I once had in my workshop, for example, was an extension of my arm. An automobile is an extension of our feet.

Essentially, McLuhan argued that new extensions take on a life of their own once they become commonplace. And when they do, we typically find that their impact is both good and bad. While my table saw enhanced my productivity when working with wood, it consumed natural resources to build and operate, was a potential source of serious injury, and contributed, surely, to my eventual hearing loss. While the automobile has given us enhanced mobility, it has also given us air and noise pollution, traffic fatalities, and an increasingly overweight population.

What about the Internet? E-mail? Social media? They all offer great benefits to individuals and society at large. But they all come with baggage. Once widespread availability and acceptance was achieved, each developed a dark side.

And so it is with scientific or deductive management. Objectivity is good. But objectivity can never exist in true isolation. Subjectivity is always lurking around the corner.

Deduction has given business the appearance of rationality. But it has marginalized induction and doubt. And in so doing it has deified the false dilemma fallacy, a fallacy further reinforced by the digital nature of modern technology and the aura of youth and wisdom it has bestowed on all things digital.

Perhaps the biggest drawback to a one-dimensional, deductive world view, however, is the other side of the coin of understanding and tolerance. It is a world of angst and anxiety. Once you cross the sweet spot on the inductive/deductive continuum, the reassurance of knowledge ultimately evolves into the stress of the perceived possible.

If you have kept up on the news of late, what one impression has come across the strongest? We are a nation divided. And we are angry and unsettled. We aren't discussing anything. We are chanting. We are turning our backs. We are marching in the streets.

My point is not to argue who is right and who is wrong. But does it really matter? Are our choices really limited to the false fallacy of either/or?

Throughout human history almost every society (in fact, I can think of zero exceptions, but I will hedge my bet ever so slightly) has explained reality, in part, through spirituality. Belief in a God or gods precedes the Greeks themselves. Even magic and superstition are deductive attempts to label that which is inexplicable in the language of science.

Can it not be said, therefore, that the petri dish of human existence has empirically—scientifically—established the human need for induction?

Twenty-Eight

Indieduction

Every good book, from the driest scientific tome to the most creative novel of fantasy, must have a takeaway. So I will give you one, just in case you don't already have one.

As I considered the content of this book, an obvious question emerged: Which is the better form of logic to apply to business—induction or deduction? The final answer: both.

The Social Styles Model, now used ubiquitously by American business, was first developed in the early 1960s by two industrial psychologists, John Merrill and Roger Reid. It is a methodology for assessing how people work and interact by assigning positions along an XY axis measuring responsiveness and assertiveness.

Graphically, the result is assignment to one of four resulting quadrants: *Driver* (high assertiveness, low responsiveness), *Analytical* (low assertiveness, low responsiveness), *Amiable* (low assertiveness, high responsiveness), and *Expressive* (high responsiveness, high assertiveness).

There is, of course, no right or wrong quadrant to be in. In theory, this is simply who you are and how you interact with others. The key to your effectiveness in working with others, however, is the third dimension of the model—your versatility. How well do you move among the quadrants in response to the predominant social style of the person you are working with and presumably want to influence or collaborate with?

I believe the same versatility should apply to your ability to move from deductive thinking to inductive thinking and back again. The most successful leaders are those who have the ability and the inclination to move fluidly from one form of logic to the other.

Deductive thinkers like scientists and engineers are naturally inclined to believe that deduction is infallible. Everything can be explained by science or algorithms. To their way of thinking, inductive logic only exists because not all truth has been deduced yet. Induction, in other words, is a stopgap measure.

But it isn't. Why does it take a man and a woman to reproduce? It's not a particularly efficient way to propagate the species. At the very least, it consumes a lot of resources. But whether you are an evolutionist or a creationist, your answer to that question is ultimately inductive. It requires a leap of faith.

What about science itself? It presumes the validity of certain physical, metaphysical, and mathematical laws. But why do those laws exist? What makes them valid?

The truth is that if you believe that science alone can answer every question, you simply haven't asked enough questions. It can't, not by a long shot.

Nor can business succeed in the ways that matter solely through commercial applications of the scientific method. Business is but a microcosm of life, a world within a larger universe. Neither is that simple. Neither the lives we live nor the universe in which we live them can be understood through deduction alone.

The twentieth century is often defined as the management century. Consultants and academics increasingly pushed the notion that effective management could be analyzed, taught, and learned, which, in turn, suggests that effective management can be objectified, if not quantified.

It is a decidedly deductive conclusion. It relies on evidence. And it presumes such evidence is, in fact, both accurate and complete. There are no gaps.

A holistic view of business in the twentieth century, however, would argue otherwise. If effective management were discoverable and so easily transferable, why do so many companies continue to fail? And why do the industries of business publishing and consulting continue to prosper? If effective management is discoverable, why has it not been discovered?

Deduction, by definition, suggests that a final destination exists. It implies a state of understanding where all questions have been answered.

The answer is that such exhaustive discovery is a false assumption. Management is no more thoroughly discoverable than love or happiness. We can deduce a directional path to achieve these things, but we cannot experience the light at the end of the tunnel without a willingness to leave the tunnel.

Do you remember the 1939 musical fantasy produced by Metro-Goldwyn-Mayer, *The Wizard of Oz*? In one of the climactic scenes, Dorothy, the lost girl from Kansas, and her friends, Scarecrow, Tin Man, and Lion, discover the wizard behind the offstage curtain. The almighty Oz, of course, is revealed as a fraud, but his very human impersonator, played by Frank Morgan, gives each of the three friends what they were searching for. The scarecrow gets a diploma and is suddenly smart, the tin man gets a heart-shaped watch and is suddenly caring, and the lion gets a medal and is suddenly brave. Each gift was tangible and its purpose—it's cause and effect—was deductively sound.

When it came to fulfilling Dorothy's wish to return to Kansas, however, no amount of deduction would suffice. As Dorothy noted, "Oh, I don't think there's anything in that black bag for me." Her wish could only be satisfied inductively through the magic of hope and desire.

The same is true in life and business. Some problems can be resolved deductively. Purely objective analysis can provide many answers. The scientific method and its variants are sound, as far as they go.

Not every answer, or every insight, or every effective decision, however, can be deduced. We must often make a leap of faith into the world of induction. We must go beyond the tangible actions of deductive conclusion and follow the beam of light sound induction shines before us.

Deduction is the logic of action. Induction is the logic of principle and context. Both have their place. The best outcome and the most effective outcome will be achieved when both are pursued in harmony and balance.

Deduction most certainly has its place in the quiver of the effective leader. It is the tool the effective leader will reach for most frequently. Danger comes into play, however, when the effort stops there, when the leader deduces a conclusion and acts on that conclusion without first subjecting it to inductive scrutiny.

Here is the simple process that I recommend:

1. Gather all of the data you can find.
2. Deduce a conclusion based on that data.
3. Make sure you can articulate the deductive logic you relied upon.
4. Step back and view the issue holistically.
5. How do you "feel" about your deductive conclusion? Does it sit right with your instinct?
6. Whether you answer that question in the affirmative or the negative, explain your answer in deductive terms.
7. If you can do that, you have either affirmed your initial conclusion or flushed out an alternative that deserves further study.
8. If you can't reconcile your deductive and inductive conclusions, start over. Ask more questions. Chances are you are pursuing the wrong line of reasoning and will make a mistake if you continue down that path.

The key is that steps two and five must be independent of each other. You must be certain that inductive logic doesn't cloud your deductive reasoning and that deduction does not overpower your inductive instincts. Achieving that separation is easier said than done and is the step in the process where most leaders fail.

That is why I inserted the letter *i* into the more logical but admittedly fabricated "indeduction." The induction and deduction cannot taint or compromise each other. They must be *independent* of each other. It is this purity, and the ability to reconcile the two conclusions, that is at the heart of managerial effectiveness.

Once again there is a parallel with the Chinese notion of yin and yang. Induction and deduction are not opposing forces. They are complementary. One cannot exist without the other in the world of effective management.

And this is where the Social Styles Model may have some application. You must step out of your box to effectively reach a sound deductive conclusion or a sincere inductive conclusion. More often than not that means stepping diagonally. If you are inclined to be analytical, you must become expressive. And vice versa. If you are a driver, you must become amiable. And, again, vice versa.

In fact, I think a fundamental rule of effective management is warranted here: Don't stay in your quadrant. Move around.

Which is why I am always wary of business people who identify themselves as "data-driven," or who proclaim, "I like to get all of the facts on the table and make a decision." More often than not, these individuals are, in fact, excessively inductive in their decision making. Consciously or subconsciously, they feel a need to hide it.

In the same vein, particularly creative individuals sometimes have to throw an anchor to windward when their creativity is applied to everyday problems. As much as I admire, even worship, creativity, it doesn't always hit the mark.

As I have noted throughout the book, nothing exists in isolation. Everything happens within a context. And it is that context that gives a problem and its solution three dimensions. Deductive solutions are often two-dimensional. It is the affirmation of induction that provides the third dimension that validates the other two and gives them the depth of conviction.

An analogy might be the use of both the left and right spheres of your brain. The whole is greater than the sum of its parts. The balanced solution is more effective than any one-dimensional solution could be.

Indieduction is the center of gravity between science and philosophy. It is where all logic meets and finds its most effective and attractive expression. It is the figurative and literal center of the circle of reason and the tangible reality it ultimately defines.

Conclusion

It is increasingly self-evident that the United States, and the world of business that so extensively shapes it, has marched along the axis of deductive logic to the point of lost equilibrium. And the only potential solution is not to double down but to seek to restore some sense of balance. That, of course, will be much easier said than done.

The world of business has a unique opportunity—and profound need—to restore a sense of balance in how we conduct commerce and employ our citizens. Business leaders, both established and aspiring, however, must first align on that need. With consensus, corrections can be made that will benefit individuals, businesses, society, and the economy as a whole.

This will ultimately require all of us in business to step back from the precipice of isolated self-interest. We must begin to measure our individual reward in more collectivist terms. Individual success is not sustainable if the tide is not raising all boats in the harbor.

The government cannot bring about this equilibrium. The people who govern have too many vested interests. It is simply unrealistic to expect those who govern to abandon those out-sized personal interests in the interest of the common good. In a world of social media and the 24-7 news cycle *noblesse oblige* is not a workable model.

Business leaders can, however, step back from the precipice. And the reason, I believe, is really quite straightforward: it is in their self-interest. With a restoration of tolerance and optimism and an acceptance of ambiguity, employees will be energized and engaged. Costs will be shed by the bucket load. Creativity and innovation will soar. Companies will flourish. And investors will be rewarded.

Any deductive analysis based on the empirical evidence of history may not offer a lot of promise for success, but that does not mean it can't be done. In the end we simply have to want it enough, to accept that not everything can be explained through the reason of cause and effect alone, that choices are not limited to the digital limitations of either/or, that collective perspectives do benefit the individual in the end, and that optimism and tolerance are the hallmarks of a life well lived.

Gary Moreau has more than four decades of experience—including twenty-five years as a C-suite executive—and has provided leadership at multinational companies throughout the world, including North America, Europe, and Asia. He lived and worked in China for nine years. Recognized by World Economic Forum as a member of the inaugural class for Global Leaders for Tomorrow (1993), Moreau has written six books (two under the pen name Avam Hale) and served on four corporate boards in the United States and Canada. Today he consults and speaks on leadership, strategy, and Asia. He is married and lives in the Midwest.

Made in the USA
Columbia, SC
09 May 2018